SUN RA

COLLECTED WORKS VOL. 1: IMMEASURABLE EQUATION

SUN RA

COLLECTED WORKS VOL. 1: IMMEASURABLE EQUATION

EDITED BY ADAM ABRAHAM

PHAEL8S

BOOKS & MEDIAWERKS

www.phaelos.com

CHANDLER, ARIZONA

SUN RA: COLLECTED WORKS VOL.1: IMMEASURABLE EQUATION — Edited by Adam Abraham. Compiled by James L. Wolf with the assistance of Robert L. Campbell, Allan Chase, Graham Connah, Ken Ellzey, Chris Funkhauser, Hartmut Geerken, Peter Hinds, Gilbert Hsiao, Trudy Morse, Steve Ramirez, Anthony B. Rogers, John Szwed, and Chris Trent. Copyright © 2005 Phaelos Books. All rights reserved. Published by Phaelos Books. Chandler, AZ 85225-8104 Email: info@phaelos.com

Sun Ra photos courtesy, Alton Abraham Estate

www.phaelos.com

Publication Date: November 2005

FIRST EDITION

Printed in United States of America

Library of Congress Cataloguing-in-Publication Data

Abraham, Adam, 1951- (Editor)

Sun Ra: Collected Works Vol. 1, Immeasurable Equation

p.;cm.

POETRY

ISBN 0-9700209-7-X

1. Poetry. 2. African-American. 3. Jazz.

2003207020

Dedication

To Alton E. Abraham (1933 - 1999)
Mystic, Foundation Builder, Believer, Space Traveler,
Citizen of the Universe...
Dad.

Words, words, words

Made fresh, made again

The recreate, the recreation . . .

The word was made fresh

Thus is the cosmic reach

Dark meanings brought to light

See the mystery...

Table of Contents

Index of Poems

Index of Poems, Cont'd.

Index of Poems, Cont'd.

Index of Poems, Cont'd.

Index of Poems, Cont'd.

LeSony'r Ra a.k.a. Sun Ra

May 22, 1914 - May 30, 1993

Foreword

Sun Ra's Spiral Poetry

Sun Ra's poetry has hardly been read, studied or argued over by anybody at all, much less by those within the realms of recorded scholarship. Still largely ignored by fans of Ra's music and even less widely disseminated than his rare Saturn records, it was seemingly intended for a larger audience than it ever got. During the late 1960s to early 1970's a poem or two, sometimes more, was printed on jackets of the more widely distributed Sun Ra records. Beginning in 1972, many Sun Ra record jackets referred the curious to a Chicago address from which was available copies of *The Immeasurable Equation*, proclaimed source (though not always) of the poems. However, most attempts to write to that address received no response. I know of only a handful of seekers who were successful. Consequently, until now the only real audience for the poems has consisted of close Sun Ra friends, experienced Tone-Scientist-Musicians, new Arkestra recruits, or the very odd fans who really dug the concert teasers/sermons about altered destiny and other worlds, and who somehow managed to pick up a book of poems at an Arkestra show. Most likely, those who own copies of even one of Sun Ra's four published books could not be numbered more than a few hundred.

Naturally, there has been little scholarly work, even of amateur origin, published about Sun Ra's poetry. Fortunately, one of these few works is Brent Edwards' excellent, *The Race for Space: Sun Ra's Poetry* (*Hambone* 14 - Fall 1998). Starting from a poem Sun Ra wrote for the moon landing of July 1969, Edwards looks at Ra's concept of the Impossible as a significant aspect of Ra's relation to the Black literature of the 1960's. Edwards then takes a wide survey of some of Ra's "modes" of poetry, such as humor, didacticism, nightmare visions, and invocation, as well as some of Ra's linguistic quirks. He finishes with a closer view of Ra's recombinative strategies—the tinkering with, and reversals of certain aspects of language, both spoken and written. These practices are helpfully distinguished from other related practices in African American literature. The essay is a perfect introduction for those who really want to engage Sun Ra's writings in their history, their intent and their possibilities.

I was first introduced to the wealth of Sun Ra's poetry by Trudy Morse, who in the last years of Sun Ra's life on Earth would sometimes take the stage to perform his poetry to the accompaniment of the Arkestra. One day in 1996 I met her in person at a Sun Ra memorial concert in Washington D.C. and agreed to drive her to New York City for another memorial concert. At the end of the trip, she gave me a copy of *The Immeasurable Equation, Volume II*, the largest of the poetry volumes. I read this tremendous gift right away. With just over one hundred poems, it gave me more than a taste of Sun Ra's linguistic spirit. It presented, bit-by-bit, the true depth of his thought and words—what he was really *about*.

I was first struck by the fact that his poems are so bravely and unabashedly *un-poetic*. I know of no poet who uses fewer concrete nouns than does Sun Ra. Take a quick glance through this volume. Wisdom, dimensions, endlessness, potentials, blackness, source, word, world, etc… are abstractions all. Two barely concrete words reappearing every now and then are *bridge* and *crossroads*, signals of what Sun Ra is presenting to us in his volumes, crossings from one place to another, points of intersection where changes of direction become possible. Beyond these two, there are almost no moments in his entire written corpus that could be called "images" which suggest visual, sonic, or tactile scenes or experiences.

The question arose, and will again for others, is this really poetry? Is this philosophy disguised as poetry, just as Sun Ra's music is "Images and forecasts of tomorrow/ Disguised as Jazz?"[1] These distinctions don't seem to have been very important to him. According to Trudy Morse and John Szwed (author, *Space Is The Place: The Lives and Times of Sun Ra*, Pantheon Books), Sun Ra read his philosophy as if it were poetry, a sentence here, a page or two there.

The next thing I noticed about Sun Ra's writing is that, as much as in his music, he seemed to want to undo and rewrite every commonly accepted concept he could get his hands on. This constant striving for conceptual liberation and reinscription resonated not only with my interest in esotericism and my amateur reading of Jacques Derrida, but mostly with the main string of my persistent if semi-naive anarchism, the sort that has run through a certain minority of white American males since at least the middle of the last century.

While Sun Ra was no anarchist of any sort, his concepts of discipline are so alien to the disciplines of our corporate-controlled world that they feel like what freedom might be if it existed. Ra often told his band members that they were in one jail or another and as long as they were with him they were in the Ra Jail. Sometimes it still seems that the Ra Jail must be the best anyone has yet thought of.

As my interest in the poetry increased, I decided I wanted to find and read it all. At the time a community of Sun Ra scholars, fans and collectors were active on the Saturn list-serve. Among these were Robert L. Campbell, Allan Chase, Graham Connah, Ken Ellzey, Hartmut Geerken, Peter Hinds, Gilbert Hsiao, Trudy Morse, Steve Ramirez, Anthony B. Rogers, John Szwed, and Chris Trent who shared and sometimes donated original copies of their poems to me.

I want to take this opportunity to acknowledge and thank them once again. Because of their cooperation and generosity, I did get to read every poem and noticed along the way that Sun Ra was a perpetual reviser of his own poems. Some even occur in three or more versions through the years. I indexed the poems with their sources and cross-referenced different versions. I also, hoping to publish the work someday, transcribed everything to word-processing files. I am happy and honored that this work made possible by the Sun Ra community can finally see light and that Sun Ra's poetry can be brought to the public as he wished it to be. I wish I could have done more, such as dating the composition of more poems and coaxing out more unpublished work. But I am glad that at last, thanks to Adam Abraham and Phaelos Books, the present book can stand as the first volume of Sun Ra's complete published poetry and prose.

I want to conclude with one last observation about Sun Ra's poetry. He is obviously very interested in undoing common oppositions, usually making the point that socially constructed "reality" is not the "real" reality. The inner becomes outer, the false true, etc. But one opposition Ra is loath to undo is that between the circle and the spiral. The circle in much esoteric literature, the sort the Ra read heavily, was often given privilege as a symbol of the Universe, Infinity, God, or whatever Final Being was first, highest, deepest, greatest in whatever hierarchy. From Ancient Egypt (where the circle was the hieroglyph of the sun) to H.P. Blavatsky and beyond, the circle is the supreme abstract geometric expression of Deity. But in many of his poems you will see Ra oppose to the circle the *spiral* as the superior abstraction of something like divinity. This again is not unique to Ra. Even the composer Stockhausen is fond of the spiral as an image of divinity, especially as it can also symbolize the musical spectrum, which curves back on itself in octaves as it rises and descends. But for Ra the spiral is much more than a symbol of divinity, musical or otherwise. It is an icon of trajectory. It goes somewhere else. It is a symbol of the path toward *alterity*, of a rising beyond the limitations of the earthly sphere (or circle — he explicitly equates the two in some poems), towards the genuinely unknown. The spiral, rising in degrees, mimicking the shape of the circle, but adding another dimension. I believe that Sun Ra was expressing through this figure his hope that even while we seem to be trapped in our earth-bound life and our fate (and he could be as deterministic as any) we *can* find or are already in the process of finding a way out that leads to something better.

From his published writings of the mid-Fifties onward, Sun Ra had a deep hope for something better, for himself, for his people, for the planet. It was never the announcement of a simplistic Hegelian inevitability, something which critic Nat Hentoff once accused Ra of hawking, but a hope that hinged on the kind of work Ra did to bring about his musicians' full potential and to show us all some-thing new in sound and spirit. It also hinged on us listening. At times, especially towards the end of his life here, his hope faded. But even his prophetic rage at our insane human race was another expression of his desire that we at least begin to become what we should always have been able to be: something impossible, other and better than what we have been for so long now. Some race of angels to whom the laws of mankind no longer *need* to apply, to whom impossibility is merely a challenge, to whom the evils of our or any world are unknown. This hope and desire is for me Sun Ra's true heart and his greatest gift to us. I hope it makes its way to you. — *James L. Wolfe*

Footnotes

[1] From the poem "Jazz in Silhouette" (c.1958), taken from the jacket of the Sun Ra LP (Saturn LP205) and CD (Evidence ECD 22012-2) of the same name.

Introduction
"His Majestic Insignificance"[1]

Some comments on Sun Ra's poetry

Sun Ra's mother was very large when she was expecting Herman and everybody thought she would have twins; but it turned out to be just a Gemini, "a disguised twin of tomorrow".[2]

Harmut Geerken

Toward the end of his life Sun Ra, who had at one time been called Herman Poole Blount, had grown a goatee beard and dyed it red. This cosmetic treatment is well known in anthropology. In Africa, in the Middle East and in India extraordinary men dye their beards red in order to sensitise themselves for their mission and their way on earth.[3] Sun Ra had known his mission as well as his path on planet earth only too well since the fifties but perhaps, in his resignation to old age, he wanted to make sure once again.

The fact that the poems of Sun Ra, the musician, can finally now be published is an important step towards a better understanding of this unique artist of the last century. There have been many thinkers and artists who have turned their backs on Western civilization (Nietzsche, Schopenhauer, Gaugin) but Sun Ra has catapulted himself more radically than the rest out of this Western atmosphere which has brought so much disaster to this planet through politics and religion. His vehicle was the myth. Without making any concessions, Sun Ra has freed himself of everything not having anything to do with the infinity of outer space right up to the holy cow of Western culture, technical perfection. Whether a record was scratched, cracked or stayed in the same groove, it never bothered Sun Ra, as long as the music had that magical quality, an indispensable parameter he demanded of any music worthwhile listening to. Correspondingly, his lyrics are different from anything Western culture was accustomed to. Until recently, only insiders knew that Sun Ra was not only an exceptional musician but also an inspired poet and a serious philosophical writer. In 1983 already, Sigrid Hauff had drawn attention, in great detail, to the literary works of Sun Ra.[4] Her essay 'Extension Out'[5] from 1994 was a first inventory and interpretation of his poems in publications and on record covers.

Sun Ra's 'magic' language is not only apparent in the rituals and call/response passages on LP's but also in the roughly twenty publications entitled *The Immeasurable Equation* and other untitled publications between 1972 and 1995. Just one glimpse into the poetic world of Sun Ra is enough to confirm that we are dealing with a unique mediumistic talent. "Ah, the magic of words... Best not let them touch you./There is poison on the blade."[6] These are dangerous words, as dangerous as some kinds of music (and maybe some writings), which Sun Ra held well away from public view because he did not consider the people mature enough. The philosopher Ernst Marcus, a distant relative of Karl Marx, had withheld his work on eccentric perception because he considered it too dangerous for the feeble-minded public. Again and again, there are obviously people who "do not consider the earth their home but the sun. Ultimately, they do not see the sun as being above them but the earth below them".[7]

In an Arabic restaurant in Cairo, Sun Ra was treated very impolitely by a waiter. He probably thought the dark-skinned Sun Ra was from Upper Egypt. In Cairo, the people of this region are often treated very arrogantly. The waiter sort of slammed the plate down on the table. Sun Ra got very angry and wouldn't calm down. He left the restaurant and went to a different one. The next day he had a gig at the El Boko nightclub. Before starting the concert he swore at the Egyptian audience in no uncertain terms. Then he sang: "This is not my people in Egypt now …".[8]

".= aim/ . = end/. = period/ . = time/ . = era/ . = age/ . = cycle"[9]

The jacket of my LP "The Antique Blacks"[10] shows the stronghold of Western culture, the Acropolis. There had been suspicions earlier on but, since Martin Bernal's "Black Athena",[11] we know for sure that the Ancient Greeks, i.e. the cradle of our highly praised Western culture, were under the strong influence of Egypt even if the die-hard traditionalists do not want to know. Roughly spoken, Ancient Greece, in a way, was nothing but a watered down and degenerated Pharaonic culture with a high level of development in regards to mythology, astronomy, medicine etc. Compared to the impressive Old-Egyptian buildings, the Greek temples seem like pastry cook's architecture. The Gods were also remodelled. Amon became Zeus, Thoth[12] became Hermes, Isis became Demeter, Horus Apollo. Quite a number of the Pharaohs were black Africans: "The Antique Blacks." In "Blackman" June Tyson sings, "*When the Blackman ruled this land, Pharaoh was sitting on his throne — I hope you understand…*"[13] There is much evidence for the fact that the high culture of the Dogon in today's Mali is descended from the people of Pharaonic Egypt. So, Sun Ra knew how he had to organize himself on this planet. Although he had landed in the Western World landing place: Birmingham, Alabama, he was well aware of the fact that his other leg was in Africa and the high culture of the Nile.

The disgraceful experiences he had in the prisons and detention camps of Jasper (Alabama) and Marienville (Pennsylvania) during the forties for refusing—as a musician—to serve on active duty, were a further reason for him to withdraw himself more and more and to escape from the world. His only refuge was in not recognizing any human and worldly things and following visions of those ancient kingdoms, where beauty was still unharmed; kingdoms in the earth's most distant past and on the "happier star"[14] light-years away.

Sun Ra's poetry consists of visionary gropings in utopian kingdoms and he only touches on worldly things for the sake of negation. "Oh! Nothing earthly…," is how the poem *Al Aaraaf* by Edgar Allen Poe begins. Just like Poe in his mythical poetic description of a "happier star," Sun Ra can only describe his longing for the impossible and a rational description of how the soul fights and tries to free itself from the earth and tries to glide into the outer spaces of the omniverse.

Sun Ra's poems do not indicate a positive understanding of history. To him, and he is not the only one to see it in this way, history was an obvious lie, an illusion, deception and imagination in the interaction of power and opportunism. The worldly so-called truths are not the ultimate resort.[15] History is not written down but invented, created and faked: "The manufactured history … The manufactured history!"[16] "The past is a fabrication thing/Some fictitious one-dimension fantasy."[17] Sun Ra prefers to rely on myth and mystery. He disassociates himself from the history-believing homo sapiens and proclaims: "His story is history, but my story is mystery!" For Sun Ra, myth is a means of experience, far away from Western rationalism and a means towards a holistic explanation and an order of things.

Sun Ra was changing his clothes and Salah Ragab happened to notice that he was wearing a gun in a shoulder holster tied across his chest with a belt. Asked about it Sunny said that he always wore a pistol and did Salah not know that he was a 'wanted man'?[18]

> *"Earth is erth … you plainly see./Revelation mystery!/Saga deep of planet three!/ … Gamma … Gamma … Gimel … Gee!!!!!/Ab the orb … octaveity/Bro to bar infinity ………!"[19]*

Sun Ra's literary work has different outputs. What can be heard in concerts and on records together with music are on the one hand call/response elements, which have found their direct way from Africa into the New World[20] and the conjuring up of ritual elements.[21] On the other hand there are the sung songs[22] which, through constant repetition, generate strong magical energies and counter energies. On paper, without music, Sun Ra creates something resembling contemplative poetry, often articulating sociocritical implications. He also uses the language of the mystics for these texts.[23] Meister Eckhart & Nikolaus von Cues (Cusanus) followed a similar path of spirituality. The thousand-year-old language and intonation of the Siberian shamans often suggests itself, as well[24]—texts which Sun Ra allows to run parallel to his thoughts are often written in the form of a recitation or a proclamation[25] or continue in a kind of self-contemplation.[26]

More of interest to me are the poems that one could assign to the area of concrete poetry, because they work with language as a material. They are texts relying exclusively on language, where language speaks for itself and where changing one single letter moves the text to somewhere else ("nation/notion,"[27] "enright/inrit/enwrit,"[28] "told/tolled,"[29] "will/wheal,"[30] "wood/would"[31]). There are different words with the same or similar pronunciation ("right/write/rite"[32]), "god's gods or God's gods. /God's God's and God's god or God's God"[33]) and there are permutations, known also in the concrete poetry of the fifties and sixties.[34]

New word coinages are typical of Run Ra's lyrics. Above all, the nominalism of adverbs, prepositions, pronouns and past tenses of verbs is striking (tomorrowness, themness, isness, thisness, oneness, backness, whenness, ifness, two-wardness, the in etc.). Some of these language oriented poems have phonetic qualities and what one had thought to have properly identified by ear for decades turns out to be an acoustic illusion in the written form, like June Tyson's declamation "a world … a world …. a world" turns unnoticeably into "a whirl …. a whirl…"[35] Here, only the typography makes Sun Ra's profundity obvious.

Finally I would like to draw attention to a group of Sun Ra's linguistic texts in poetic form. Language is taken to pieces with a dissecting knife,[36] examined for logical or suspected references,[37] expanded or compressed mercilessly,[38] vaporised into child-like word games[39] or put side by side polaristically.[40] Sun Ra was often out to be not understood. The incomprehensible always remains a mystery and the impossible, which may become possible was of crucial concern to him.

When Sun Ra was in Cairo in 1984 with the Arkestra, they lived in a big flat in the Zamalek quarter. One morning around 4 a.m. Danny Thompson phoned up Salah Ragab and asked him to come to Zamalek immediately. "Don't ask!" He set out at the crack of dawn and when he got there, he saw that a camel had been slaughtered in the street right in front of the house where the Arkestra was staying. Everywhere was pouring with blood. It was an offering from a rich man for the poor and the slaughtering has to be finished before sunrise, in accordance with Islamic law. Sun Ra and the members of the band were very upset and shocked. They had been woken by the screams of the people and the camel and could not understand what was happening.[41]

"What/How/Which/Where/And/That/So/If/Those/Then/Me/Them/Why?"[42]

What Sun Ra has in common with other philosophers is the striking formalism of the language. His texts resemble the vague hermetic statements of Martin Heidegger as well as the crystal-clear formulated, polaristic linguistic equations of Salomo Friedlaender. I have tried to point out the amazing similarities between Friedlaender (1871-1946) and Sun Ra on a double CD with the Art Ensemble of Chicago.[43] Friedlaender's philosophical journey takes us to the center of human existence and to the sun he wishes to see at its center, in keeping with the Copernican worldview. "Zero sun" is a constantly recurring term in Friedlaender's philosophy, depicting the center, the origin of coordinates, the zero, the "0" of human existence. This center is inviolable as the sun and represents a "majestic insignificance." Were it not, our existence between the poles might be worn away by the trivialities of day-by-day life.

From this indifferent zero, creative processes can be initiated. Sun Ra's "no point,"[44] on the other hand, has utopian characteristics (Greek: u = no & topos = point; utopia as the place of no point). His philosophical itinerary describes the 'nowhere-home' of outer space by leaving the earth far behind ("this planet is not my home"). Sun Ra moves as naturally in the omniverse as do mere mortals between the suburbs of their hometown. Although Friedlaender and Sun Ra have followed opposite directions in their thinking, they arrive at the same destination. This is apparent even in the titles of their works: the *I-Heliocenter* of Friedlaender and Sun Ra's *Heliocentric Worlds*, or Sun Ra's poetic work *The Immeasurable Equation* and Friedlaender's polaristic opus *Schöpferische Indifferenz* (Creative Indifference) or *The magic I* (Sun Ra) and *Das magische Ich* (The magic I) by Friedlaender.[45] These analogies, however, are not intended as proof of congruence between the two philosophical systems. Yet it is a fact that both of them stem from a deep dissatisfaction with the state of the world: Friedlaender the Jew, in the era of the Holocaust, Sun Ra, an African/American in a society distinguished by a repressive intolerance. Friedlaender and Sun Ra have drawn their conclusions by declaring the earth a meaningless battleground which they rise, self-assuredly, above, assessing the world by their own standards from an individual state of suspension (Friedlaender: "Only by floating can one trust the abyss"), and refusing to acknowledge death (Sun Ra: "Give up your death!" Friedlaender: "I am the death of death").

Friedlaender's main concept of the balance of the extremes was formulated by Sun Ra in a very similar manner: "the beautiful sameness of opposite direction-destiny;"[46] "I like the counterpoint to a central theme."[47]

Friedlaender was an expert on Kant and quite obviously Sun Ra has also concerned himself with Kant. His poem "Thing in Itself" refers directly to Kant's "Ding an sich"[48] (thing in itself). Kant's famous statement that mankind gains by losing can also be found in Sun Ra: "If we fail, we must win."[49] — I do not know how well Sun Ra had read Kant. The "incorrectly" quoted German expression of the "Ding an sich" (from Sun Ra the "Ding and sich") could lead one to assume that Sun Ra adopted Kant in a similar way to Chopin[50] and Rachmaninoff[51] — not in an analytical way, word by word, note by note but spontaneously, freely, intuitively and light-heartedly with regards keeping to the original and without worrying that the original may have been meant in a different way.

In the area of philosophy Friedlaender and Sun Ra seem to have achieved what physics and biology have been working on intensively for years: a kind of cosmic formula about life and the world which can be employed to harmonize the individual, society, science, politics and art. They see the central point in different places, places that are extremely far apart but at the same time, closer together than one might think. Sun Ra sees the central point "many light-years in space," a place maybe only he, as *The Chosen One*, has experienced. Friedlaender, on the other hand, analogous to the Copernican revolution that puts the sun in the middle of the solar system, developed a philosophy which puts an inviolable central sun inside man that, through its polar force field, makes everything outside revolve around this 'I-Heliocentre' like planets.

When I drew Sun Ra's attention to Friedlaender in a hotel bar in Cairo in 1971, he was very quiet and detached and did not really want to hear what I was trying to tell him, in my enthusiasm, about this philosopher who was so close to him. Probably this closeness was too obvious and put him off. Which of us likes to hear that somebody else is working with the same terminology!

Trudy Morse was with Sun Ra on his deathbed. Unfortunately, because of Sun Ra's distant relatives, she had no possibility of freeing him from the undignifying life support machines. Trudy was at his bedside in the hospital, reading him his poem, "This place is not my home". He wanted to say something but was no longer able to articulate himself intelligibly for human beings. He made some kind of animal-like sounds. His eyes began to glow bright red like burning coals.[52]

"Once/Never upon a time/Twice Twice/You will see that thatness/Thereness ….. Theirness ….. themness."[53]

On the day I started to write this text, the postman delivered a book of Ilse and Pierre Garnier titled Poésie Spatiale.[54] Something happened that has happened so many times when I was dealing with the phenomenon of Sun Ra: coincidences which would take pages and pages to describe. — The beginnings of the space poetry of Ilse and Pierre Garnier go back to roughly 1963. "We used to live protected within our own air coat. Now we are like waves shooting about in the universe."[55] The language of magic does not start out from the idea that words were invented by human beings but that "they were given to us, like hands and the stars… each word is an abstract image. — A surface. An expanse."[56] The space poetry of the French couple Garnier does not mean an enclosed space but the absolutely open-ended space that Sun Ra called at roughly the same time, "outer space."

Sun Ra's poems untie language following the recipes of the dadaists, the structuralists, the lettrists, the futurists and the cosmologists. Above all, his poetic texts consist of energies. Sun Ra did not write because he wanted to communicate thoughts but because he cultivated particular vibrations and frequencies from which the texts emerged more or less automatically and spontaneously. The reader of Sun Ra's poems "enters a wild and free world, a world without a pope, without kings, without religion, and without refuge. He becomes a tree, a bird, a dancer, a barque, a wave — parts of a cosmos which creates all possibilities and destroys all certainties."[57]

When I went for a walk in the morning sun with Sun Ra in the palm gardens of the Menahouse Hotel at the foot of the Cheops pyramid there was a multitude of birdcalls from the tops of the palms. Sun Ra stopped still and said: "Can you hear them? The birds are doing what we are trying to do all the time." He saw men as "birds without wings"[58] and the terminology of his poems repeatedly revolved around the picture of the bird, of flying, of feathers, the nest, the wings. Ornithopoetry! — *Hartmut Geerken*

Footnotes

[1] The Thick Darkness

[2] The Cosmic Age

[3] Robert Lawler, *Voices of the first Day*, Rochester 1991, p. 104; see photos of Sun Ra on "Purple Night" (A&M 395324-2), Pleiades (Leo LR 210/211), "Hours After" (Black Saint 120111-1) & "Reflections in Blue" (Black Saint BSR 0101)

[4] Sigrid Hauff, *Sun Ra - Der Mythos*, radio broadcast, SWR, 1983

[5] Extensions Out in: Hartmut Geerken, *Omniverse Sun Ra*, (Waitawhile 1994)

[6] Alert

[7] Salomo Friedlaender/Mynona, Der Liebesflug, 1928

[8] According to Salah Ragab

[9] Words

[10] The Antique Blacks (Saturn 81774)

[11] Martin Bernal, *Black Athena - The Afroasiatic Roots in Classical Civilization*, London 1987

[12] For a while the Saturn label was renamed Thoth.

[13] Thoth.

[14] Edgar Allen Poe.

[15] Beyond the Truths.

[16] The Invented Memory.

[17] The Past is like a Dream.

[18] According to Salah Ragab.

[19] Of the Planet Earth.

[20] Nuclear War.

[21] Black Myth/Out in Space (MPS Motor Music 557656-2); I, Pharao (Saturn 6680); They plan to leave (on Saturn 10-14-85 & 91983-220)

[22] To Nature's God; We Sing the Song To; On Jupiter.

[23] The Empty Space.

[24] The Differences.

[25] Discernment.

[26] Disguise.

[27] The Endless Realm.

[28] The Enwrit.

[29] Every Thought is Alive.

[30] The Spontaneous Mind.

[31] The Tree is Wood.

[32] The Enwrit; Detour.

[33] Men and Amen.

[34] "Tomorrow Never Comes; Freedom versus Black Freedom."

[35] Strange Worlds on Black Myth (MPS Motor Music 557656-2) & the poem "The Go Round."

[36] The-O-Logy.

[37] The Crate Create.

[38] The Inned Inning.

[39] The Tree is Wood.

[40] "Circle Eternity;" Angels and Demons at Play (Saturn 407).

[41] According to Salah Ragab.

[42] Sins of Not When.

[43] Hartmut Geerken and The Art Ensemble of Chicago, zero sun no point (Leo LR 329/330).

[44] The No Point

[45] Salomo Friedlaender/Mynona, Das magische Ich, Bielefeld/Germany, 2001.

[46] Equality: parallelism.

[47] The Empty Space.

[48] Thing in Itself.

[49] Fabricate.

[50] Prélude in A major, op. 28, N. 7 on Pleiades (Leo LR 211) & Queer Notions (DIW DEP 1-1).

[51] Prélude in C minor on Aurora Borealis (Saturn 12480)

[52] According to Trudy Morse.

[53] And Some Music.

[54] Ilse and Pierre Garnier, Poésie Spatiale/Raumpoesie, Bamberg/Germany 2001. Garnier's manifestos about spatial poetry are reprinted in Pierre Garnier, Spatialisme et poésie concrète, Paris 1968. About terminology and tradition of Spatialism see David W. Seaman, Concrete Poetry in France, Ann Arbor 1981, p. 229-286

[55] Pierre Garnier, Manifest für eine neue Seh–und Lautpoesie. Les Lettres/Revue du Spatialism 29, 1963.

[56] ibid.

[57] Gerhard Penzkofer, Introduction to Poésie Spatiale/Raumpoesie, Bamberg 2001.

[58] Sun Song; Birds Without Wings.

Preface

All photos courtesy, the Alton Abraham Estate.

My Music Is Words

Some people are of this world, others are not. My natural self is not of this world because this world is not of my not and nothingness, alas and happily, at last I can say this world is this unfortunate planet. The destiny of this planet is at stake, one fatal further mistake can cause its long delayed destruction. One fatal mistake can be its last mistake. The future is obvious, but the potential impossible is calling softly and knocking gently . . . calling softly to the natural selves of nothingness according to the standards of infinity nature and infinity nature's BEING . . . . knocking gently upon the door of those who are of nature and nature's God.

There are other dimensions and the equation of it is every other world in the infinity of the universe. This is the why of the music I represent; and this is the why of the image of a better world: the alter-life for the alter-life is different from the life of this world. This is a mean world, and by the same token, it is a poor world, poor in spiritual values, void of natural contact with the natural-infinity/otherness Being.

Suddenly, now is different from the once I knew and the things I do and say are of necessity a magnification and at the same time a nullification of calculated myths and vicar-images. Nature . . . intuition . . . psychic harmonization . . . NATURE . . . INTUITION . . . PSYCHIC HARMONIZATION! LIVING SYMBOLS OF DISCIPLINE . . . happiness for and from the greater universe.

Because of segregation, I have only a vague knowledge of the white world and that knowledge is superficial; because I know more about black than I do white . . . I know my needs and naturalness . . . I know my intuition is to be what is natural for me to be . . . that is the law of nature everywhere . . . there are different orders of being and I call upon the forces of nature to witness that I have written and I have said that no order has a right to infringe upon the rights of another order of being, for each order has its own way and weigh of being... just as each color has its own vibration... My measurement of race is rate of vibration-beams . . . rays . . . . Hence the black rays is a simple definition of itself/phonetic revelation. I do what I have to do according to my natural order of being because that is how it has to be and at the same time that is why. That is why and because; because in the scheme of things, even the least of brothers has his day and when you realize the meaning of that day, you will feel the presence of an angel in disguise. If an angel led the exodus out of Egypt, why can't an angel lead some others somewhere else. Consider: what is the value of a dying world? Or even the life of it, if that so-called life is cruel meaninglessness . . . ? If you do not understand anything else, understand this . . . that the least of the brothers in his humbleness and understanding of the weakness and the strength of everything is the initiator and the interpreter of the dimensions of the infinity . . . and that is why there is a black angel race of beings or soul-mates.

Freedom to me means the freedom to rise above a cruel planet. FREE-DOM TO ME MEANS THE FREEDOM TO RISE ABOVE A CRUEL PLANET AND TRUE PROTECTION IS PROTECTION BY THE BROTH-ERS OF NATURE AND NATURE'S GOD . . . INFINITY EVERNESS... ["]The lifting up shall be the casting down," and it is written that he cast upon them in his anger and fury "a band of evil angels." . . . My words are the music and my music are the words because it/is of equation is synonym of the Living Being . . . darkness upon the phase of the deep . . . the face phase . . . the eye of infinity . . . black equation from and of the angelic is . . . the immeasurable ARE.

When I speak of freedom, I do not speak of the freedom of the land of liberty or the freedom of any land of this plane of existence, for this plane of existence is only a temporary illusion . . . shadows and images that sometimes intermingle with the delusion sent for "he sent upon them a strong delusion in order that they might believe a lie;" but and then, there is more than one lie.

The tree of the knowledge of good and evil is forbidden as far as the fruit of it is concerned but so is the tree of life. What price forbidden fruit and forbidden trees to those to whom it is forbidden? Did you ever see a voice walk-ing? If you didn't, it is probably because you did not realize the meaning and significance of the word the voice.

These are indeed perilous times. They are perilous to every man, woman or child . . . If the white race chooses to ignore that warning it is already of the past . . . Yet even now I feel a great pity for those who may not listen before it is too late . . . . Never comes tomorrow . . . comes tomorrow never . . . tomorrow comes never . . . never tomorrow comes . . . tomorrow never comes . . . comes never tomorrow . . . there is always the alter-fate . . . elastic spiral potential infin-ity discipline other planes myth reality.

What is this world to me? It is truly nothing; I have sought to bypass it rather than to become a part of it, because it has no known diplomatic relation-ships with the Creator Creater of the infinity universe. The truth concerning this planet is indeed dreadful to behold, how strange it is that the truth should reach the state of the dreadful!

Yes the truth is that the truth is bad as far as this planet is concerned. The neglected mathematics of MYTH is the equation differential potential impossible potential potential potential otherness alter-isness.

My music is words and my words are music. Why should only 144,000 understand? Yet if I am not of this world why should I care? There is great darkness and why not if they dare to obscure the name of the sun and why not if they dare to be rebellious, and why not if I have been abused and neglected and bypassed. My words are music and my music is words and none can understand better than the pure in heart, for they being pure know purity in any guise. If something or even nothing does not know its own kind, it is not being kind to itself.

My words are music and the music is words but sometimes the music is of the unsaid words concerning the things that always are to be, thus from the unsaid words which are of not because they are of those things which always are to be . . . . nothing comes to be in order that nothing shall be because nothing from nothing leaves nothing.

The music comes from the void, the nothing, the void, in response to the burning need for something else. And that something else is something else/this nothing, this outer nothing is out of nothing, it is the music of the spheres. The symbol for every sphere is the sign of nothing: O . . . The spiral is another type of nothing . . . it is of the onward reach.

When one is primary-young . . . all the ideas in the world converge in counsel and through disguised declarations play upon one's brain like fingers upon some tender instrument . . . then there are then the impressionable days of splendor/electric naturalness/ flash lightning touch upon the time negatives of variable universe and what one feels is better considered as the music of the unsaid words. That is one approach, but there are myriad approaches.*

My early approach to music was in recognition of all types and forms of music as being of great inportance in the scheme of order and chaos, intelligence and ignorance . . . the scheme of things, the general and the rare . . . the priceable and the priceless. To me all types of music are music but all types of music are not Space Music. According to my weigh of things: Space music is an introductory prelude to the sound of greater infinity. It is not a new thing project to me, as this kind of music is my natural being and presentation. It is a different order of sounds synchronised to the different order of Being.

I am the least of the brothers again as far as popular jazz is concerned, that is why I had the time to develop and discipline the outer-infinity coordination sound. Along the way I tried to interest popular Jazz musicians in the ideas I wanted to share with them so that we could be brothers in a pleasant as well as profitable sound venture for them as well as the listeners. They were not pioneers for the togetherness I represented, finally I decided to keep moving on the outward onward plane for On is synonym of the Sun . . . after all what is there better than the expression of the you in the interplay of the self and the alter-

self when the myth abstracts sound their sound.

The natural Jazz musicians I knew during my early formative years were a pleasure to know . . . they were sincere and unselfish . . . . It was always a great pleasure to hear them play for they had so many things to say in a spontaneous and natural manner, the music they played was not conventional, nor was it in popular jazz commercial form.

During my years in High School I played and studied all forms of music and the theory of the same . . . .

My relatives liked Bessie Smith, Ida Cox, Ethel Waters and other Race artists and they always took me to the theater to see and hear the Race artists perform whether they were great or small.

I believe that the first Jazz record I ever heard was by Fletcher Henderson, his records were a part of the record collection my relatives possessed. Later I added Duke Ellington, Art Tatum, Earl Hines, Fats Waller, Teddy Hill, Chick Webb, Lionel Hampton, Sunset Royals, Tiny Bradshaw, Louis Armstrong, Henry Red Allen, Jay McShann, Charlie Parker, and the other Bop greats.

Of course there were others. I used to search for everything that was new or different. There were some white bands like Boyd Raeburn and Stan Kenton until one day I found out that black arrangers were the major source of their ideas and that black arrangers and composers were BUILDING WHITE BANDS WHICH FINALLY TOOK THE PLACE OF THE BLACK BANDS WHICH FORMERLY HAD PLAYED THE TOP JAZZ SPOTS OF THE WORLD. These arrangers probably had their reasons for doing what they did, financial perhaps . . . I never got around to ask them why. I do know that the black race as a whole did not wholly support what is called Jazz, they did support blues and gospel and their derivatives. Even the Negro intellectual did not seem to understand the meaning of Jazz and its contribution to the cultures of the world at large.

I appreciate all types of music but some music I find is not conducive to my development spiritually and otherwise. Basically speaking, the giants of Jazz I mentioned earlier were the musicians I listened to as a child. They had so much to say to me that I needed to hear, and in this kind of world I found that there was no one else who could say it the way they could; because all at once when they played, there was hope and happiness and natural beauty. Then something began to happen to Jazz, the Jazz musician was commercialized and packaged and Jazz began to be a product of, and from the white world. In many cases, it was supervised at the recording sessions by white A & R men particularly during the reign of Bop. Since I was not a product of the white world, I found that I could not fit comfortably in the place they had reserved for the black musician... so I did not compromise and I did not lose my naturalness. What I am playing is my natural way of playing. It is of, for and to the Attributes of the Natural Being of the universe of which is, and it is to everything that should be is, because to me it is natural.

I have a gift to offer this planet and music is one of the bridges to the treasure house of it. I am doing what I am supposed to do, I am being what I came here to be. Those who are in tune with Nature can hear what those who are not in tune cannot hear, and then they will know the meaning of the natural beist. The space sea has many sounds of beistness. The Akasa, the unknown acoustics, the alter-planes of isness are all a part of everything, the everything and the nothingness of Space Outer.

Under terrific opposition, I have tried to show and demonstrate my goodwill to the world, simply because I know this can be a better world for every person, people or peoples. All that I am is a visitation and that is the meaning of the natural alter-self. If you are dissatisfied with yourself in the scheme of things and the altar has not changed conditions, perhaps you should consider the alter. After all if anything changes, it will be through the word alter/alteration/alternative because how can you dare to speak of change if you do not have an alternative? The alternative to limitation is INFINITY. Yet, be warned! Infinity is precision discipline. Infinity being INFINITY is naturally of duality because and as it is written, "The secrets of wisdom are double to that which is."

SUN RA

JANUARY 29, 1968

NEW YORK, NEW YORK

The 'Father' of Intergalactic Music?

From the Editor: Reflections on Sun Ra

Sun Ra was a grand master of music whose "time" seems yet to lag behind him, years after his earthly passing. As this writer reflects on the nature of time and space, myth and race, God and Soul, and life within the Cosmos, it is an honor to acknowledge the contributions of Sun Ra. An iconoclast in the truest sense the term, Sun Ra made such topics his musical trademark, long before such ideas seemed plausible.

For anyone who doesn't know by now, Sun Ra was the leader of Sun Ra and his Arkestra (that is how they spelled "orchestra"). Perhaps they were making a play on the word "ark" which, given their point of view, would have been a reasonable way to describe the planet earth itself.

Over its lifetime several names were used as identifiers, including Sun Ra and His *Intergalactic Solar*, *Myth Science*, and *Astro-*

Adam Abraham

Ihnfinity Arkestra. From its start in the early 1950's, his group was "far out" long before it was *cool* to be that way. Not only did in their choice of outfits stand out (they could make George Clinton look conservative), so did their message. This was, and probably remains, the most cosmic *conscious* band of musicians to come down the line. To my knowledge, no music group has presented such a consistent message, before or since, about the possibilities of otherworldly existence and the importance of knowing our spiritual self. Sun Ra even taught a class on this and other topics, at the University of California, Berkeley in the early 1970s.

"The Dead Past"

The civilizations of the past have been used as the foundation of civilizations of today. Because of this, the world keeps looking toward the past for guidance. Too many people are following the past. In this new space age, this is dangerous. The past is DEAD and those who are following the past are doomed to die and be like the past. It is no accident that those who die are said to have passed since those who are PASSED are PAST. –Sun Ra

I have a personal, if somewhat oblique connection to Sun Ra and his music, through my father, Alton Abraham. He was the mastermind behind the Sun Ra persona, and founded El Saturn Records in Chicago, IL, a small record label. My father, who passed from this earth in 1999, was every bit the force behind the message of space consciousness that Sun Ra delivered both musically and in writings, to audiences around the world. He and Sonny were "two of a kind."

Formed in Chicago in the early 1950s, the group's musical style began as bebop and swing. Over a forty-year period, it evolved to define free jazz. Though they did indeed play contemporary jazz of the day, they also played what could be characterized as a brand of unstructured or freeform instrumentalism.

Sun Ra and Alton Abraham would meet in this metaphysical moment of Chicago in the 1950's. Alton Abraham, magic man of knowledge and meanings was already in Chicago, born there in 1937. An x-ray technician, Abraham was known to make predictions, a seeker of knowledge in the Bible and other arcane sources. As Alton and Sonny grew in metaphysical strength, new seekers came in their sphere. Luis T. Clarin, Lawrence M. Allen and James W. Byrant formed a research group that would be known as Saturn Research and later a corporate entity called Ihnfinity, Inc. would arise.—Len Bukowski

The young mystic Alton Abraham founded El Saturn Records in Chicago in 1956 to document Sun Ra's compositions and take them out of the rehearsal room. The small, idealistic record label was part of El Saturn Research, a group of intellectuals and musicians around Abraham and Sun Ra who studied all sorts of theosophic, scientific and prophetic texts. In El Saturn Research reports of UFOs, speculations about extraterrestrial life, science fiction and new developments in space travel were connected with prophesies about the end of the world. El Saturn Research gave a new impulse to Sun Ra's music and the Astro-Black Mythology: Afrocentrism turned into Afrofuturism. Sun Ra's outlook became more and more fixed on the future.—Ben Schot, Astro-Black Mythology, Blastitude #13.

Sun Ra "pushed the envelop" in every way. He was one of the first adopters of the electric piano and the Moog synthesizer. The band included standard instruments as alto, tenor, and soprano saxophones, trombones, clarinets, flutes, and drums. Then there were unusual items, such as a baritone sax, bongos and other percussion pieces, gongs, bells, and chant vocalizations. Their live shows included dancers and film projected onto the stage, with their bodies serving as individual "screens" in space.

> *Their headquarters would be in an apartment dwelling at 4115 South Drexel Blvd. (in Chicago), walk-up, a dwelling loaded 'from floor to ceilings with all kinds of books. Books such as deLaurence's 'The Master Key," perhaps. Or maybe Manly Hall's 'Secret Teachings of all ages'." And books on Egyptian mysteries, Schopenhauer, biblical texts, kabalistic tomes and Nostradamus were all needed. Theirs was a research center, hidden away from prying eyes. Vocalist Roland Williams spoke of these texts, these meetings. "They went deep. Came back up too. Sonny got lots of his ideas about permutations from Alton." By definition, metaphysics is a science that seeks to probe the logic of thought. An attenuation of the mind to mystical vibrations. Sun Ra and Alton were seekers with minds fully aware. Thought dynamics accessing new worlds.—Len Bukowski*

Though the group also played jazz standards such as Green Dolphin Street, and 'Round Midnight, their main interest and focus can be easily discerned in following titles: *Distant Stars, Dimensions in Time, Enlightenment, Saturn, Atlantis, Somewhere in Space, Interplanetary Music,* and *Rocket Number Nine Take Off for the Planet Venus.*

> *Alton Abraham and Sun Ra spoke of space travel, journeys to stars beyond, long before such feats were reality. Roland Williams recalled many times Sonny spoke of astral traveling to doubting listeners. Like tenor saxist Johnny Griffin, who stated, "I'm not from this planet. I did something wrong on my home planet and I was sent here as punishment," Sun Ra also believed himself to be of alien origin, proclaiming the planet Saturn as his home. The phrase 'Black Science Fiction' is in vogue these days; Sonny and Alton were well in the midst of such matters back in the day. For outer space and space travel has long been a part of Afro-American religion, music, and life: Ezekiel and the flying chariot. Such themes resonate in Black churches, themes that are a part of Alton Abraham and Sun Ra's heritage. And Sun Ra and Alton Abraham were part of the tradition. And long before George Clinton's Mothership Connection, before Sun Ra's Omniverse, Elijiah*

Messrs. Bukowski' and Schot's quotations excerpted from Blastitude #13 August 2002, edited by Cary Loren—www.blastitude.com

Muhammed spoke of the "mother Plane," a flying vessel of destruction which would herald the final war, showing the "power and wisdom of Allah."—Len Bukowski

Long before it made any sense to me, my father knew and proclaimed that we were not of this world. This understanding represents the real product that Sun Ra and his Arkestra offered to his fans.

"'The impossible is the watchword of the Greater Space Age.' The space age cannot be avoided and the space music is the key to understanding the meaning of the impossible and every other enigma."—Sun Ra

My father, who also influenced the likes of fellow Chicagoan Ramsey Lewis to transition from gospel music into jazz, created the cosmic, otherworldly theme that the Arkestra would become famous for. I personally never met "Sonny", as dad called him, but I definitely met his message, for my father was the source behind the force.

With my parents divorcing when I was around three years of age, time with my father was occasional at best. I had no awareness of his group, and little understanding of what he did to make a living (children rarely have such concerns anyway; their needs are much more immediate and basic). He certainly wasn't a postal carrier (a respected job in those days) or a factory worker. I only knew that he was gone quite a bit. When he did visit, he talked and I'd *listen*.

My dad shared with me fantastic and "far out" ideas about humanity and its evolution, and about himself and me. He said that our family members are direct descendents of the Biblical Abraham, with whom an irrevocable trust was made with God.

My dad also made it clear in no uncertain terms, that he and I had come to earth from Saturn. "Okay…", was a typical reaction that went through my mind.

Whether these statements were true or not, who was going to argue the fine points of such information? Certainly not me. Yet, although I did not ask if I could see the contract at the time, I now know, with the same confidence of my father, that each and every one of us holds the same agreement/covenant with The Source, irrespective of where we "come from."

Dad stated his rather obscure beliefs with a sincerity and conviction that led me to believe that he had some basis to work from. Fortunately, he also offered to me other points that were more accessible for my mind to rally around. For example, he made it very clear that we were "here" (meaning on Earth) to be of service. In fact, the bulk of what my father told me made sense. Throughout our lives, he said time and again, we were to be seekers of wisdom, knowledge, and understanding. We should put the Creator (God) ahead of us in all things that we do, expressing gratitude for the great opportunities that we have been given. True to the teachings of my mother and grandmother, an emphasis was always made on the importance of good deeds.

It is always better to know than to "no". —Alton Abraham

At one point in my life, like many children, I resented my father for not "being there for me" as I was growing up. I consoled myself by saying that *he* missed out on a good thing, when in truth I was likely sad that I was the one who was missing him. Nonetheless, in spite of my parents' differences, I was taught to "honor thy father and mother", and took the instruction to heart.

The resentment I may have had toward my father never overshadowed the respect that he was due, for the information that he passed to me was always of a positive, empowering, and inspirational nature. He encouraged me to seek and do great things, which resonated with a sense within myself to do likewise. Whether or not I understood what he did or was telling me, I went on with my life, and found my own Way, which Sonny might refer to as, "Weigh". Ironically, or perhaps prophetically, my dad and I now share many of the same views, with some subtle nuances. However, there is no difference in the principles that we embrace: that which is for the good of humanity as a whole.

As such, my father was clearly on the loving edge of thought, and created a great legacy by which such ideas could be safely explored, through the music of Sun Ra and his Astro-Ihnfinity Arkestra. Perhaps now I am joining him, finally.

One day, Sun Ra will be the next big "discovery" of our time, and just possibly, the man behind the man. But for now, enjoy this written collection of thoughts from a man now gone, for whom time is finally beginning to catch up.—*Adam E. Abraham*

The Key to The Immeasurable Equation

This is the entire compendium of published Sun Ra poetry, as painstakingly compiled and notated by James L. Wolfe. The poems that are included in this and subsequent volumes of *Sun Ra: Collected Works* will indicate the edition(s) in which they originally appeared.

A - The Immeasurable Equation 1972.
   Ihnfinity Inc./Saturn Research, Chicago, IL 72pp.
B - The Immeasurable Equation Vol.II. Extensions Out. 1972.
   Ihnfinity Inc./Saturn Research, Chicago, IL 144pp.
C - The Immeasurable Equation 1980. Philadelphia. 72pp.
D - The Immeasurable Equation 1980. Philadelphia. 88pp.
E - The Immeasurable Equation 1985. Philadelphia. 32pp.
F - The Immeasurable Equation 1985. El Saturn Records. Philadelphia.
   20pp.
G - The Immeasurable Equation 1985. Omni Press. Millbrae. 32pp.
H - The Immeasurable Equation 1985. Omni Press. Millbrae. 28pp.
I - The Immeasurable Equation 1985. Omni Press. Millbrae. 20pp.
J - The Immeasurable Equation 198?. Omni Press. Millbrae. 28pp.
K - The Immeasurable Equation 198?. Omni Press. Millbrae. ?pp.
L - The Immeasurable Equation 198?. Omni Press. Millbrae. 32+pp.
M - The Immeasurable Equation 1989. Omni Press. Millbrae. 36pp.
N - Sun Ra. 1989. Omni Press. Millbrae. 60pp. Sz C
O - Sun Ra. 1992? Omni Press. Millbrae. 16pp.
P - Sun Ra. 1994? Omni Press. Millbrae. 12pp.
Q - [No title]. 1994. Omni Press. Millbrae. 24pp.
R - Sun Ra Research. Omni Press. Millbrae. Issue specified.
S - Stylus (Vol.13, No.1, Spring 1971) Temple University, pp.50-55
T - LeRoi Jones and Larry Neal, eds. *Black Fire: An Anthology
   of Afro-American Writing*. N.Y. William Morrow, 1968
U - Umbra Anthology 1967-1968 pp.3-7
V - Comments and Poetry by Sun Ra. El Saturn Research. 4pp. [1978?]
W - The Immeasurable Equation. El Saturn Research. 1985. 32pp.

* Almost identical versions. Insignificant differences.

After That

After that, what is there after that?

And that afterwards is

Or doubly no The not of those things which are . . . . .

If I to be am

Then to be is and are.

Why did other voices speak to you

And enchant your mind . . . . . . ?

It is what your mind is must seek to understand

Beyond the planes of earth-light love.

And what are planes of love, if no you do not?

    Cascades of emotion: if no you do not

    shimmering ecstacy: if not is the wisdom.

I have known a heaven all my own

If others know of it

Say or if they do not to me . . .

I have seen eye to eye with every mind's eye

That I have touched vibrationally upon the planet

Without antagonistic resistance understanding always

        and

Basically why those were as they were.

How bitterly long have I searched

For all that is mine: Now I must be, I must be:

    And mine is mine . . . . .

My immortal pure idea

My sound idea

My virgin version

I came to be of

If that conception that I will to be.

Angelic Brothers

Knowledge cannot know me

And wisdom cannot describe

The delicate mystery of love

For you are my friends

I call you friends

Angelic brothers

For of the world of

That which is not to the world

The unknown-twin dimension-being.

Are you as I am Other Eternal To Be.

Be-earthed (1972)

Those who are be earthed

Are be erthed

Burthed or berthed

They are placed

In their place

Now Ge is the earth

And Gesus is earthsus

And Ge's is earth's

Ge's us is earth's us

Consider Gheez and Gheezus

Be-Earthed (1980)

Those who are be-earthed

Are be-erthed

Berthed . . . .

They are phonetically birthed in their berth;

They are placed in

In their place . . . .

Their place is their prace/praise/glory/fame . . . . name.

Now Ge is one of the symbolical names of earth,

And since that can be considered as a basic equation-form;

We might as well consider that Ge's is earth's

And Ge's us is Earth's us.

By Golly! (1972)

I always felt and

I always feel

That chance and circumstance

Of earth-bound life is nothing real.

It is not real

This life they live

Even and what

It has to give.

It is not real

This angel's folly

By heck! By Jove!

By Gosh! By Golly!

By Golly! (1980)

I have always felt

And I still always feel

That chance and circumstance

Of earth-bound life

Is nothing real . . . . .

It is not real

This life they are said to live;

Even and despite all it has to give . . . .

It is not real

This angel's folly

By heck! By Jove! By Gosh!

By Golly!

Calling Planet Earth (January 1990)

There is no need to cry
No need to be confused or
bewildered
Listen to the three of us
me, myself and I.
Architectural-equation facts
are the order of the day
There is change everywhere
The stars themselves in the
solar system must be placed
in new places around the sun.
Earth itself must be positioned
in a different place than where
it is.
Listen carefully to these words
They are not the words
that have been or was
They are the words that are, is
and am to be.
If you do wrong, you have to
pay,
But if you do right, you have to
pay too;
Also if you do nothing
You have to pay. They have
vagrancy
laws you know.
You can go to jail for doing
wrong.
You can go to jail for doing
right.
You can go to jail for doing
nothing.
You have never been told this
before
so now you know.

There is something in the
cosmos
called Fellowship. Reach for it.
If you want a better way/weigh
It is quite more sensible
and more profitable to pay
in advance to join the cosmos
fellowship,
Some people call it "dues".
If you pay dues for something
worth
infinite value you will get
what is due you on an
infinite eternal plane of being
compensation: so valuable
there is no
place to measure its worth.
Thus I have spoken
and thus it is hereforth
written in the stars.

.

Challenge

It is another age, another challenge
A greater one than ever faced before
In all of Nature there are changes everywhere
Subtle but insistent
With immeasurable potentials for good or bad
It is all according to, or the interpretation thereof
Whichever ever they choose
Or which any way they determine to go
They will have to change
The people will have to change
Nature is changing everywhere
It is another age . . . another cycle-day
There is no place to hide
This eon:Cosmo-void
Cannot/will not be denied
It is ultra-true
There is no place to hide
Therefore, the people will have to change
The people will have to change
The people will have to change their tune
And that tuning should be in tune with the Inless outer universe
The endless immeasurable not
And this is the dual meaning of the phonetic not:note!
A differentiation note, phonetic multi-meaning sound. Note:
A tiny message wrote, a view... an idea plane of fame
A note is symboled music name of tone
A permutation change, so plain to see
That not is note and note is not
It's based upon the circle. See?
See?

Circle Eternity

Faith can be a bridge
Between what is called reality
And what is thought to be
myth
For myth is a word
And a world all its own.

Myth has attributes
Magic, impossible
Faith all sympathetic
To the word myth.

If you are not a myth
Whose reality are you?
And if you are not reality
Whose myth are you?

The pupose of life
Decree: -- death . . .
The purpose of death
Decree: -- life
The pupose of life
Decree: -- death
The purpose of death
Decree: -- life
Death -- life
Life -- death
Purpose -- aid -- end
End of life . . . . . death
End of death . . . . . . life
Circle eternity
At one ment atonement
Destiny equation
Eternity
Revelation.

Limited eternity
Purpose . . . . aim . . . . end
Purpose aim . . . . end
Man!
Citadel of etrenity*
Planes of inverted
comprehension

man! man! man! man! man!
Destiny fate
Circle of etrenity
Eternity circle
Eternity era of error
man! man! man! man!
Man!
What is this seeming life
That always seems to end in
that seeming death?
What is that seeming death
That always seems to end in
That seeming life
For it is ever that: the eight
The Eden.
The paradise where life begin
And death death.
The state of life
The state of death
Atonement . . . . . .
Onement
One . . . . .
Circle.
Eternity . . . . .
One
O . . . Perfection endedness
Endedness Endedness
In deadness

Endedness
One.
Man has become as one
Man has become as one of us
You can not stay in the garden
You can not stay in the garden
You can not stay in the garden
Of Paradise, it is a garden for
neophytes
Arise man out of your oneness
The name of one is forbidden
To you
Taboo . . . Taboo . . .
Sacred . . . Forbidden . . .
Arise man
Oneness is of confusion!
They sought to be as one
At the Tower of Babel
Beware man!
Taboo . . . Taboo . . .
Taboo . . . Taboo . . .
Forbidden
Man
Beware
The sacred name of one
Do not seek to
Usurp the name of the sacred
one
The sacred one
The sacred one
The sacred one
Beware man

* Let the centuries be your
enlightment

Read your histories
Your history of oneness
Your history of once upon a
time
Once upon a time
But before once was nothing
And after once is twice
Never before the once
And twice the presence of
never
The pleasant nothing of never
For nothing
Nothing is
And nothing from nothing
leaves
Nothing
And one from one leaves
Nothing
And two from two leaves
nothing
And three from three leaves
nothing
And everything from
everything leaves nothing
And nothing from nothing
inverted leaves
Everything
So if one sends one
There is nothing
For one from one
Leaves nothing
There is nothing in the never
land
Of Never.

---

* Might be a mistake, but since it is repeated below, it may be a play on the French "etre" (to be).
* The text from this point on was republished under the title "Once Upon A Time" in 1980.

Colors and Notes

Colors are different
As every different thing is
different
If the Lord makes a difference
in one thing from another
He has set the pattern for
other things to be different
from the other
He has set the pattern for an
other thing to be different
from a one.
There is the presence of
duality
In all it's infinite and splendid
reach
It's reach potential is
everywhere.

Colors are different as every
different thing is different
The vibratory pattern . . .
The vibratory pattern tones
are different sounds . . .
A color tone, a color shade . . .
Timbre.
And timbre's crest in heraldry
And timbre's timbre: quality.

Color's difference identify . . .
Show your colors!
Fly your flag!

Heraldry and coat of arms
Show your colors!
Fly your flag!
Yes.
Colors do identify.

You see no color?
Your world is colorless
You're color-blind!
You've failed the test.

I would not even mention this
But nature's nature is the
same
No matter what you do or
what you say,
The laws of nature have not
changed
And nature's colors, colors are
        For every color codes
it's name
Though colors bend and colors
blend
        The laws of nature have
not changed . . .

Concerning That Which Is Called Life And Death

If the death of death is life
(for how can death die unless it becomes alive?)
And if death becomes alive
Is it not active on another plane?
The life of death . . . . .
Is it not the inversion of the death of death?
Or is the death of death, the life of life
It is varied mathematics in permutation forms.

Circa 1966

The Cosmic Age (1968)

This is the Space Age
The age beyond the earth age:
A new direction
Beyond the gravitation of the past.
This is the space age.
This is the disguised twin of tomorrow
Striking upon the earth
With relentless power
Like a perpetual whip.
This is the Space Age --
Prepare for the journey!
You have a rendezvous
With the living wisdom
of the unadulterated fate.
Prepare for the journey!
Like a happy child
You will step out of the pages
of the blinding-blend of the book,
And gaze astounded at
The Endless space of the Cosmic Void.
Your new course is the Cosmic Way --
Your new vehicle is the Cosmic plane;
You will learn to live the Cosmic Way,
You will learn to journey with courage --
With the fiery aim to reach
The even greater day
of the even greater tomorrow
The greater tomorrow of the Cosmic Age.
The second main is the master key
From the heaven of Outer-Space.
The second main
Is the second principal
The principle:
Cosmic-Timelessness of the Cosmic Age.

The Cosmic Age (1980)*

This is the Space Age
The age beyond the earth age:
A different direction beyond the gravitations of the past.
This is the Space Age:
The disguised twin of tomorrow
Striking upon the earth with relentless power
Like a perpetual whip.
This is the Space age-----
Prepare for the journey!
You have a rendezvous
With the Living Wisdom
Of the unadulterated fate.
Prepare for the journey!
Like a happy child
You will step out of the pages
Of the blinding blend of the Book,
And gaze astounded
At the endless space of the Cosmo-Void.
Your new course is the Cosmic Way ----
Your new vehicle is the Cosmic plane;
You are to reach/approach the Omni-Cosmo Way
You will learn to journey with courage . . . .
With fiery aim to find
The even greater day of the even greater tomorrow . .

The Cosmo-timeless realm
Of the Omni-Everlution-Immortalic Day.

* For a third version of "The Cosmic Age", also from 1980, see "Prepare for the Journey", on page 143.

Confrontations (1972)

Confrontations?
What are they to me
Man always loses
Can't he see?
Confrontations against the representative who is a friend
Is himself at odds with himself
Man always loses
Doesn't he know?
Who always wins in the end?
It is the nameless totality,
The constant imperfection of immeasurable On.

Confrontations (1980)

Confrontations
What are they to me . . . .
Man always loses . . . . Can't he see?
It takes more than a man
To win against the ironclad
Star enfated
Chained to futility destiny.
Confrontations of man against his friend
Is man at odds with his vibration-tuned
Harmonious and kindly self.
Man always loses . . . .
Doesn't he know,
Who always wins in the end?
It is the nameless totality
The immeasureable
Ever-changing
Omni-On.

The Damning

The damning of the spirit
Is the reservoir of salvation . . . . .
Thus to save is to damn . . . . dam
Like water in a damned condition
Is water reserved . . . .
Hence comes power from the damned
Yes, from hence comes power from the damned
Behold! See the mystery of the curse-oath
Oath-curse-binding promise-damn dam . . . .
It is written: "The first shall be last" . . . . . .
Celestial interpretation code revealed:
"The first shall belast" . . . .
Bemuse this fact and bethink
Upon its namification.
If it is to see to know . . . . . .
The Cosmos Omni told me so.

The Delusion Freedom

It is not right
>For those to speak to me
>>Who speak of love,
>If they have never felt
>>>The meaning of Love.
It is not right . . . . . . it is oh so wrong!
So very inexpressibly wrong!!!
For those to speak to me
Who speak of freedom
Whose freedom is liberty-will of wisp
 What good is freedom's liberty
>If sword and famine and pestilence
>>Is its creed . . . . . . It is according to
That which is written
>As proclaimed word of God
>>To those to whom it was given:
An unfailing promised heritage.

Love and freedom,
What words are they!
>God is love they say . . .
The events of the world
>Are the fruits thereof today . . .
Is this life all that life should be?
Is that why the tree of life
>Is denied to those who by disobedience died
Who deadened by the forbidden knowledge
Would be twice alive . . . .
Freedom is a hidden code-delusion-key.

Circa 1966

Discernment

When we speak, we speak profoundly
And break the mirror
Of the glass through which the shadows
Were discerned
And taken to be models
From which to pattern
And to become alike to,
Alike to shadows in a mirror
What justice is this?
Indeed what justice is this?
When humble content
Is taken to mean cowardice
When humble content
Is taken as a signal to break and abuse the spirit.
And what spirit is this?
A division should be made
Concerning that which is spirit.
It is not right to force different spirits to be one
When one is distortion
And the other is clarification
Is this justice, just is,
The status quo, the maintained principle
Of the dead past
Or is this justice, just is only.

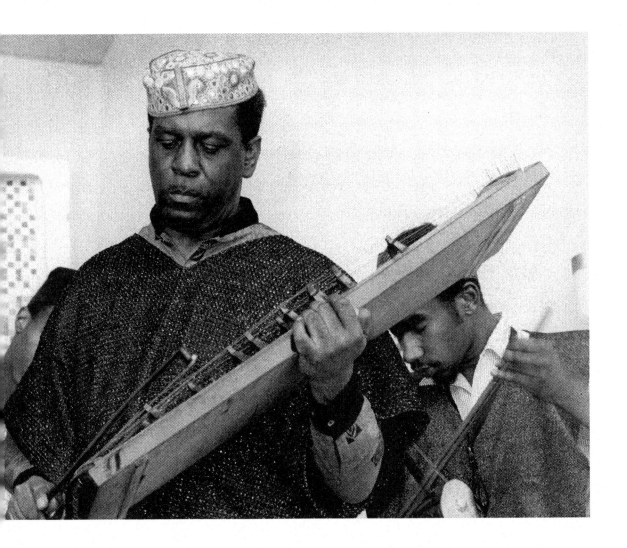

The Empty Space (1972) *

The airy heaven is the empty space
The division of heaven is inner and outer
The limited heaven is the inner
The outer heaven is endless heavens realm . . . . .

The third heaven of the heavens is called earth
It is heaven # three
The earth is as the beginning
It is the foundation of itself
It is an o
Or a o
Which is the alpha omega of the material plane
Yet every planet is an o
But earth is ao #3
Or the third o from the sun.

The inner air from another plane
Is like the counterpoint to a central theme
The enclosed vibration limitation
Repeats itself over and over . . it is a cycle . . an eternity never
changing
The outerspirals move brilliantly with word-precision, yet varying
Ever outward and ever onward on.

* For a 1980 version of this poem, see "The Heaven # Three", next page.

The Heaven # Three* (1980)

The airy heaven is the empty space . .
The division of heaven is inner and outer,
The limited heaven is the inner.
So you see there is more than one heaven.
The third heaven is the area heaven #3
Which is the material plane called earth.
The earth is as the beginning;
It is the foundation of itself . . . .
It is an o
Or a o
Which is the alpha omega
Of the material plane.
Yet every planet is an o
But earth is ao # 3
Or the third circle from the sun . . . .

The air from another plane
Is like the counterpoint to a central theme.
The limited sound: the enclosed sound
Repeats itself over and over . . . . . .
It is a cycle: An eternity never changing
And there is nothing new under the sun there.
The limited eternity is different
From the outer spirals . . . . .
The outer spirals move brilliantly
With vivid precision . . . . ever varying . . .
Ever outward and ever onward . . . .

Disguise

I can feel who I am
I do not disguise myself to me;
. . . . . . Why should I?
I have known me longer than anyone else
   I shall continue to know me
     More than anyone else;
We have been together so long . . myself and I
I should always say we instead of I . . .
We instead of me.
Because we can feel that we are we.
Others guess and think they know
But they do not feel the essence-ultra
Us of we.

We do not know we know
We only feel that this is so . . . . . .
Our intuition is the alter-being:
The entity vital-seeing: Our intuition is
The vital-seeing . . . The entity alter-being
I can be me for them . . only as they see me . . .
And not as they think they feel;
For they seem to feel another way of thought:
That's not my way.
Although we are me
The is of us is I . . .
We are more than three:
There's us and me . . . we and I
We are more than three
There's I and we

   Us and me.

The Endless Realm (1972)

I have nothing
Nothing!
How really is I am . . . .
Nothing is mine.
How treasured rich am I
I have the treasure of nothing . . . .
Vast endless nothing
That branches out into realm beyond realm.
This and these are mine
Together they are nothing.

The idea of nothing
The notion of nations
Nation . . . . notion

I have the treasure of nothing
All of it is mine.
He who would build a magic world
Must seek my exchange bar
In order to partake of my endless
Treasure from my endless realm of nothing.

The Endless Realm (1980)

I have nothing
Nothing!
Nothing is mine.
How treasured rich am I
I have the treasure of nothing . . . .
Vast endless nothing
That branches out realm beyond realm . . . .
This and these are mine;
Together they are nothing.

I have the treasure of nothing,
All of it is mine.
He who would build a magic world
Must seek my exchange bar
In order to partake of my endless treasure
From my endless realm of nothing.

Fabricate

If we fail, we must win

Victory in defeat

Because the answer to the problem

Is the defeat of the problem

And this is the black revelation

Whence the blackness

The blackout,

The blackout is the reign of the blackness

And therefore the rain

Drop and blackdrop of darkness black

Backdrop

Whence the lifting up: The casting down

The casting down: The lifting up.

Motion?

We besecond the be, for we are two and

others.

Code:

If we fail, we win

And when we win we win.

The Fantasy (1972)

I am not a fantasy in a real sense
I am a fantasy of differential-projection
Yet I exist . . . .
There are no shadows where I am
Because I am the fire of the lightnin
And the flames of the sun.
My name is the sun
I am the stranger
From the sky
Far away farther than the eye can see
Is my paradise
A mythical world
In Outer Space.

The Fantasy (1980)*

I am not a fantasy in a real sense
I am the fantasy-image of the differential projection,
Yet I do exist
Twin in spirit-being . . .
Yes, ... I am here but I am also there
Some far off celestial dimension there . . . .
Some omni-splendid myth--world's there.
Alien I?
But I am a spirituel-sun
Alien I? . . . . Why?
  Stranger I ? . . . . Why?
    How can I be an alien to you unless I feel that
        You are an alien to me?
Yes . . . I am a spirit-stranger from the sky
Far away . . . . . farther than the eye can see
Is my paradise
A mythical world
In Outer Space . . . .

The Flesh (1972)

The word that was made flesh was made fresh
It is the new, the new test .. the new tester, the test-tester-testament
The testament new
Words, words, words
Made fresh, made again
The recreate, the recreation . . .
The word was made fresh
Thus is the cosmic reach
Dark meanings brought to light
See the mystery
Hear the sound duplicity
The double opposite parallel
Hear the sound duplicity
The double opposite parallel.

The Flesh (1980)

The word that was made flesh was made fresh
It is the new, the new test .. the new tester,
The testament new . . . . reiteration of words
Words . . . words . . . a world of words
Reiterated . . . proclamated, illusionated
Devious truths .. blessings of glorified doom
Thusly and verily and Behold! I say unto you ..
Words .. scenarioed as a tale that is told . . . . .
Of thus it is written, "We live our lives" . . . . .
The word-world of words . . . . Made fresh ..
Made again . . . the recreate . . . the recreation . . . . .
The word was made fresh . . . . .
Thus is the cosmic reach:
Dark meanings brought to light . . . .
See the mystery!!!
Hear the sound duplicity . . . . .
The double opposite parallel . . . . .
  Yes, hear the sound duplicity
  The double-opposite parallel . . . .

The Flesh (1980-version 2)

Israel . . . . . . Is Ra El? . . . . . Ra Is El . . . .
El is Ra . . . .
L is R . . . .
Flesh is fresh is new . . . .
The word that was made flesh was made fresh
It is the new . . . new   test . . new tester . . . . . .
New Testament . . . The testament new . . . . . .
The Word . . . words . . . . words made fresh . . .
   Made again . . . . . The recreate . . . the recreation
   The Word was made fresh . . . . . .
   Thus is the Cosmic reach . . . .
   Dark meanings brought to light . . . .
   See the mystery
   Hear the sound duplicity . . . .
   The double opposite parallel . . . .

Tomorrow's Realm (1972)*

In some far off place
Many light planes in Outerness-Space
I'll wait for you.
Where human feet have never trod
Where human eyes have never seen
I'll build a world of otherness . . .
Other-abstract-natural design
And wait for you.

In tomorrow's realm
We'll take the helm
of a new ship
Like the lash of a whip we'll be suddenly
on the way
And lightning-journey to
Yet another-other-friendly shore.

* See also "In Some Far Place" and "The Far Off Place" for very similar poems. This version may be the earliest of all, since it contains the same key words as, but differs the most from, the other versions and their final incarnation as the lyrics to "I'll Wait For You".

In Some Far Place*

In some far place
Many light years in space
I'll wait for you.
Where human feet have never trod . . . .
Where human eyes have never seen,
I'll build a world of abstract dreams
And wait for you.

In tomorrow's realm
We'll take the helm
Of a new ship . . . .
Like the lash of a whip
We'll be suddenly on the way
And lightning-journey
To yet another friendly shore.

The Far Off Place*

In some far off place
Many light years in Space
I'll wait for you
Where human feet have never trod
Where human eyes have never seen
I'll build a world of abstract dreams
And wait for you.

In tomorrow's realm
We'll take the helm of new ships
Then like the lash of a whip
We'll start on our way
And safely journey to another world
Another world -- another world's world.

* See also "In Some Far Place" and Tomorrow's Realm" page 30, for similar poems.

The Inned Inning

If through the once to the in
　　　　　You are onced as the inned
　　Upon the time one
　And one time one time one
　Time one time one time one
　Time one is equal the 1'd of the past,
　Then you've been had by one.
　　　　Because one time one time one
　　　Is still one . . there is no change
　　　It is monotony
　　　Which is timed one of itself . . . .
　　The 1-ed: the 1-de . . the I.D.
　　The knowledge/id/idea
　　Of good and evil or good ind evil . . . .
　Because the and is the an
And the n and the ind is the n and the in
Thus the en is end and ind the inned . . . .
Entered in . . . interred-interment . . .
Yes the n is the en is the in is the n . .
If the three is as one then one is as c;
But when it is onced it is threed
And thus treed because the tree is three

　　The trio/three of the tree so treed is seed
　　The revelation of the seed is thriced
　　Once and for all understand this:
　　Through the once to the in, one is onced in
　　Inned into the eternity cycle one onced
　　　　　trio treed ceed seed c'd.

Intergalactic Master (1972/80)

Full age is [of][1] different connotation

Symbolization from[2] the void

Immeasurable fullness

Feeling determinant

Full age

Is of the priceless treasure

Above eternities

Full age

Is the feel of things

And Intergalactic Master Control

[1] The 1972 version does not contain this word, but the 1980 does.
[2] The 1972 version has "form" here, and this seems to be corrected, rather than revised, in the 1980 version.

The Farther (1972)

Get over into the spirit of things
Thus the movement is on.
The science of ontology
Is the science of the spirit
Because spirit is always of the "on"
Quality
Ever moving toward
The farther place or the
Place of the farther
Which sight is the "I"
Because the eye is the sight;
So that the sight of the Father
Is the scene or seeing of the Farther.

The Farther (1980)

Get over into the spirit of things
Thus the movement is on.
The science of ontology is the science of the spirit
Because spirit is always of The On
Always moving toward the farther place:
The site of the farther
Whose sight is the "I"
Because the eye is the sight
So that the scene or seeing of the farther
Is the site and sight of the father . . . .

The Garden Of Eatened (1966)

Alas, for those within the Garden of Eden
The Eden Garden
The Eating Garden
Necropolis: the Eating Garden
Where bones and flesh of the inhabitants are Eaten.
THEY ARE IN THE GARDEN
They are gardened
Since they were taken they were gottened
And gardened
Planted like a seed
In the Garden of Eaten.
They are the chosen ones
The begottened begardened
In their place of berth.

The Garden of Earth (1972)

Alas, for those within the Garden of Eden
The Eden Garden
The Eating Garden
Necropolis, The Eatin' Garden
Where bones and flesh of the inhabitants are eaten.
They are in the Garden,
They are gardened
Since they were taken (wrested), they were gottened
And gottened/gardened
    Planted like a seed
    In the Garden of Eaten
    They are the chosen ones
    The begottened begottened begot
    The begottened begardened
    In their place of berth.

The Garden Of Eden (1980)

Alas, for those within the Garden of Eden
. . . . The Eden Garden . . . .
The Eating Garden
The Eatened Garden
Necropolis . . . . . The Eatin' Garden
Where bones and flesh of the inhabitants are eaten.
They are in the Garden
They are gardened since they were wrested
. . . . Now they are sayed to be rested/at rest . . . .
They were taken by the taker under   . . . .
They were wrested and rested by some force
. . . . Whose power is it's weakness
By which it weakened them . . . .
Yes, They were taken . . wrested . . . gottened
Begotten . . . begottened/begardened
Now they are in the garden of eating being eaten . . . . .
Thus is the meaning of the Garden of Eden . . . .
. . . . It seems that the word Eden is used as a synonym
Of the word Paradise, ...
Paradise is sayed to be a Persian word meaaning:
A fenced in garden . . . .
Lo . . . They are planted like a seed
Down in the garden of eating being eatened
. . . They are the chosen ones
. . . The begottened begardened
Restin' in their place of berth . . . .
. . . . They were borne
To their place of rest
It is a backward version of birth
Which is better stated as a re-birth.
A rebirth is a being born again . . . .
. . . . A cryptic word of crypt-intent . . . .

The Glory of Shame (1972)

Neither honor nor despised
and rejected state crave I
When honor is deemed by law
To be the glory of shame
The tree of evil,
The tree of good?
Of evil good
Of good evil?
The tree-------the tree is three
Gamma-Gimel-G
Gamma-Gimel-X
A drama on words
See the play?
How evil is good
How good is evil
When standards cross
Upon the cross of the earth.

The Glory Of Shame (1980)

Neither honor nor rejected state crave I

When honor is deemed by law

To be the glory of shame . . . .

What price glory?

Seek not the place of glory

Until glory is gifted to be a different-equation story.

Behold! . . . The drama upon the tree

A drama on words . . . .

See the play?

The tree is three . . GIMEL . . . . GAMMA . . . . GE.

Ereth is eerth is earth is erth is thre is three.

The earth is the third planet from the sun . . . . .

Can you doubt it is three? . . . .

The Go Round

Circle turning in the sky . . . . .

Round and round it goes . . . . go round

Circle turning in the sky

Third in sun-space verity

Permutation dirth as three

Very, very, verily

      Irdth is earth

        'Tis plain to see . . . . . .

Dirt is earth?

    Oh yes, my dear !

    The truth of that is plainly clear . . . .

Circle circle in the sky

Round and round it goes . . . go round . . .

      Perhaps, that's why

      They call it ground

        Because they can see it

         Round go-round . . . . . .

   Round and round in a whirl

      Perhaps that's why

      'Tis called

      A world

        Because it's always in a whirl.

  Round and round it goes . . . . awhirl

   A whirl . . . a whirl . .

        A world . . . awhirl . . . .

God Wot (1972)

God wrote in code, He did, he Did!
God wrote in code. He did . . . He Did
His act, He did: enactment thus
His code He did his word
He did, he did . . He did his word whose code he hid.
The where and whence of some do know
It's in the sure . . . . It's in the sho'
The sure and show
Straight from the shoulder
Frankly so
Earth itself is shore . . . is shore and shoulder shore, its
shoulders show
The yes of it is testament
A show . . . . . . A shore
A showdown EVIDENT . . . . . The evident is evidence
Point of decision demand command
The showup scene, a voice-word spoke
The revelation probe . . . broke code . . .
The showup scene was mean, was mean!
The showdown time
Did let you know
That God's word
Is always sho'.
Don't you know, it's surely sho'
Raise your hands and testify . . .
Do you believe?
Now answer: "sho'"!
Answer "Sho'"!
The show is spoke of openly
It's always frankly thus, you know, you see. You see?
Sho' you know!
You know you know
YOU KNOW.
Sho' you do.
You know you know.

God Wot (1980)

God wrote in code.
   He did!
   He did!
  His act He did . . . . enactment thus
  His word he did to execute
  Perform He did that appointed to!
  In secret--code His word he hid . . . . .
  A play He made upon the word!
  He sealed the word and made it law!
  A certainty
  Of surety-sure
  Fulfilment sure . . A word made good!
  Sure and Sho' . . . straight from the shoulder
  Frankly so! Earth itself is shore. it's sho'
  Earth itself is shore and shoulder sho'
   Its shoulders show . . . . . .
   The yes of it is testament.
   A show . . . a shore
   A showdown evident . . . The evident is evidence!
   Point of decision demand command . . . .
    The showup scene . . . a voice-word spoke
     The revelation code . . . broke code . . .
    The showup scene was mean, was mean!
     The showup time did let you know
      That God's word is always sho' . . .
    Raise your hands and testify . . . .
     Do you believe?
     Now answer: "Sho'"! . . . .

The Grass Grew Tall

The grass grew tall----------
Across its tips,
The wistful winds blew gustily;
And sang the strange luring songs
That touched the heart,
And enchanted the mind.
The wistful winds blew
Like words from some strange throat
Piercing the invisible walls
Of dimensions beneath the slanted sun of earth.
The winds blew wistfully;
And I felt
That all the years were as the sand
Upon the shore of a vast sea,
That whirl and whirl
Never again to rest upon the shore . . . . .
Whirl and whirl
With growing intensity:
All the years . . . . . .
Whirling and cleaving together closer and closer,
Until they become as one . . . .
     And
         With a soft bewildered cry
            Fly out to sea . . . .
       That vast sea that has no end . . .

    . . . .

Here Am I

Here I am,

I say what I say;

And they say what they say.

Here we are;

Yet they say they are

And I am not.

Here I stand.

Yet I am not

A living, breathing myth-

For those who can see

The meaning of the magic lie.

I Deal In Souls (1972)*

I deal in souls
The stuff of which dreams are made
More delicate than finest lace
More valuable than all the precious gems in the world.

I deal in souls
Tender souls
Souls yet reaching in search
Souls of spiritual growth
Who feel themselves strong
I mold them with my fingertips
(tho' they are unaware of this)
I shape each to be a separate part of each
And yet complete within itself.

I deal in souls
I make them to become nearer to what they seek
I make them to become nearer to what I seek
This double destiny
more precious to me than written words
(more precious to me than futile sounds
        of vanity from traitorous lips)
I deal in souls I see them as they are
And not as they pretend to be.

I deal in souls
It is not amiss that I speak to my prized possession
It is not amiss that I speak
Words which are strange to the world
But which have deepest meaning to every soul
That hears my voice
And listens intently
To the things
I do not say
Rather than to what I say.

The Soul Dealer (1980)*

I deal in souls
The stuff of which dreams are made . . . . . .
Priceless souls Tender souls
More delicate than finest lace
More valuable than all the precious gems
In the world

I deal in souls
Souls reaching out to be
Souls of spirituel growth
Souls yet reaching in search
Who begin to feel the weakness of strength
And the strength of weakness.

If thus they be
I mold them with my fingertips
Whence beams of sound project
Rays of Cosmo-energy-sun . . . .
Tho' they are unaware of this;
I shape each to be a separate part of each
In discipline-ownness

I deal in souls . . . I make them to see
    The intermingled-double-destiny
    Is what they need to seek
    The gift I bear
    Deep hidden riddles brought into the sun
    So that all can see there are greater truths
    To feel and know . . . . I deal in souls . . .
    More precious to me than written words
    More precious to me than futile sounds
      Of vanity from traitorous lips

I deal in souls . . I see them as they are
    And not as they pretend to be.

I Have Forgotten (1972)

I have forgotten.
I had to forget
The yesterday way,
The yesterdays path . . .
I seek
I seek
A better place
Not like the plane of the one dimension paradise
The one dimension Babylon,
The one dimension one!
Not like the place of shame confused with glory.

I seek a vaster realm than that
Or this
I seek a vaster realm of profitable enlightened vision,
A region-realm of chromatic truths, truths of alter-reality, yet . . . . . .
Abstracts of living-cosmo design
Full of warmth and planes of light from other worlds.

I Have Forgotten (1980)

I have forgotten.
   I had to forget
     The yesterday way,
       The yesterday path

I seek a better place in the sun:
Not like the planes of the one dimension paradise
     Or one dimension Babylons.
Beware of one dimension-one
Enter not into the place
Of shame confused with glory!

I seek a vaster realm than that or this . . .
I seek a celestial realm
  Of profitable enlightened vision:
A region-realm of chromatic truths . . .
    Truths of alter-reality
         Yet
Omni-abstracts of living cosmo-design,
      Full of warmth
    And ultra-planes of light
      From other worlds.

Flight (1972)

What I thought I am
I am not
What was and is
Is not
What dreams were mine
I am not
What was and is
Is not
The laughter, the tears
The fleeting years
Like pages read and turned
Are not
Gone like a sigh
Or a bird swift
In sudden flight

I Thought I Am: Am Not (1980)

What I thought I am
I am not . . . .
What was and is
Is not . . .
What dreams were mine
I am not
The laughter
The tears
The fleeting years
Like pages read and turned
Are not
    Gone like a sigh
    Or a bird swift
    In sudden flight . . . .

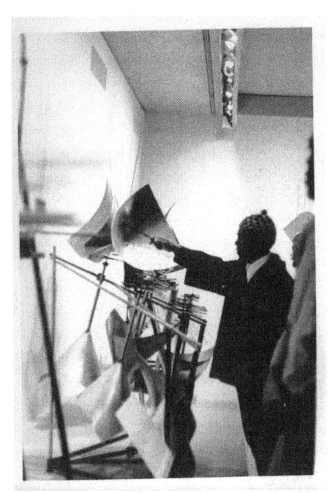

Circa 1966

I/We

And their world was beautiful.
I cannot describe
The then of it;
Where now remember I nothing more
Refulgent or greater in enduring love
Of them only are we left,
For I am we:
Their themness.
We see us
Of the world of transient notness
And treasure the world they knew
As a heritage rare . . . .
Although, I thought
We had forgotten.

If I Told You

If I told you , "I am from outer space",

You wouldn't believe a word I said.

Would you? . . . Why should you?

You've lost your way . . . . . .

You should have nothing to say.

You've lost your rights

To walk on Jupiter and Mars.

And even other worlds unknown among the stars

Among the stars.

You've lost your rights to the pleasant

To the pleasant things of being.

You've lost your rights,

Your cosmo-interplanetary-intergalactic

    Eternal-rights of Celestial being.

    Hark!

    This existence is not what it seems.

    True, it is of the truth, it is existence;

    Yet and still . . it is not being . . .

    If it were of omni-being, it would be.

    And what is called life

    Could be seen from a different view

    To be enclosed in an abstract-prism

              Haven-heaven-hell

    For shades and shadows

    Of the inner darkness.

Ignorance

The attributes of ignorance

Deserve consideration

Ignorance, an exalted state among men, abides:

Thus Ignorance is said to be bliss.

The equation: Ignorance equals bliss

Deserves due consideration.

The power of ignorance

Must be given credit for its activity

A temple to the god of ignorance

And the guardian creator of confusion

Should be built.

Is ignorance a blessing or a curse?

Consider the merits and demerits of ignorance.

Illuminates (1970)

sound radiates
illuminates
articulates the symbol of
and* what it radiates it is

on what it illuminates
it casts the touch of fire.

* The 1980 version has "On" instead of "and".

The Image Reach (1968/72)*

To
The territory of the non-memory
The realm of the moving potential
of that which is not --
To
The state beyond the image-reach
The magic life of myth
And fantasy
I speak
And say "Welcome."
I welcome thy presence
As a very Cosmic gift
of sheer happiness.
The happiness I have known
Are no longer mine.
I cast them to the world
And say "Take these"
As you have taken all else from me,
For I have one foot upon
The threshold of other realms
And wings
[Have grown
Upon my mind
To take me
Beyond the gravity
And gravitation
of the earth.]

* The lines in brackets are not in the 1968 version in Black Fire. The quotations marks are taken from the 1972 version. While not ideal, these marks make better sense than those in the 1968 version, which may have been altered by Jones/Baraka et al.

The Image Reach (1980)

To the territory of the non-memory
The realm of the moving potential of that which is not . . . . .
To the state beyond the image-reach
    The magic cosmo-life of Myth and Fantasy
        I speak and say "Welcome."
      I welcome thy presence as a very Cosmic gift
Of sheer happiness beyond sublime.

The happinesses I have known are no longer mine,
I cast them to the world and say,
"Take these, as you have taken all else from me,
For I now stand upon the threshold of other worlds
And WINGS have grown upon my mind to take me beyond the
        Gravity and gravitation of Earth. . . . .".

Imagination

'Imagination' is a magic carpet
Upon which we may soar
To distant lands and climes
And even go beyond the moon
To any planet in the sky

If we came from nowhere here
Why can't we go somewhere there?

* A later version of "Enticement" of 1957. "Imagination" was recited in the 1968 recording "Somewhere There"
and later published several times.

Immortals

Yesterdays
    and
        tomorrow
           are
       different
When they exist in their own spheres
      but when every tomorrow is the
         same as every
yesterday
      Then, that every tomorrow is not
        the real tomorrow
        Because it is only a copy of
all the yesterdays gone by.

The Immortals

They live endlessly
Who have no end
And their end is their aim
Thus immortality
Being the state of endlessness
Is because of thought
differentials
The state of aimlessness
The point is the aim
Thus: "."

The Imperative

They turned this way and that; then laughed
For they were like a thing encaged,
Too sad to sing-----------
And they had heard that laughter
Is a way to song and joy.
They've turned this way and that and sighed
That they should be a thing encaged:
Too tired to live-----------
For they had heard that sighing
Is a way to ease a grief.

Come song, come joy, come grief
Their laughter and their sighing
Have naught to do with these.
Life has its ways
And it is imperative that they should know
What makes them what they are.

In Human Form

In human form
We have so much to expound
Yet even more
So much more to learn;
So much more to be . . .
To understand.
In human form
Imprisoned we
But yet another greater dawn
Will give us being invincible
Upon the planes
Where life is not life
And death is not death.

[Interpretation]*

Interpretation is not without its value.
When it's equational . . .
It can nullify extinction . . . . . .
It can even bypass the truth
And things of earth as they are and was
Will fade from the mind as if it had
      Never been.
The hand that fate dealt earth
    Should never have been allowed
      Within the scenario
        Called "life"

* This poem without a title appears on the same page as "Like Seeds", p. 68. It might be a second part of "Like Seeds", but this does not seem likely. Neither poem appeared in any other publication.

The Invented Memory (1968)

What is called man when first created was
given an invented memory:
A storehouse of manufactured, unschooled
conceptions,
conclusions and beliefs.
These conceptions, conclusions and beliefs
were placed in the
minds of what is called
man, in order to keep
same from looking
backward into a void .
. . Because of what has
happened.
The word man is but an
image-symbol
Thus man is striving to
be the idea of himself.

The pattern of the
model-man is the idol
which man worships
Without understanding
why and without seeing
the end-product
Which is the conclusion
of the finished man.
It is finished refers to
the conceptions of man
And likewise the
conception.

Conceive is to think
Or to become pregnant
with:
Thus the riddle of the
version is no longer
virgin.
The manufactured history . . . The

SATURN RECORDS, P. O. Box 7124, Chicag

manufactured history!
How came the manufactured history?
Because of the void . . . The manufactured history was
substituted for the void in order to keep man from feeling empty
And without foundation.

The real truth is that a man is but the blueprint or image of a
house.
And now he must build himself to be the reality
Just as he builds his house to live in, he must build himself to
Live in.

Must he use the foundation of the substitute for the void
Or must he use a greater type of wisdom
Older than the void and splendid in the Cosmic sense?
This is the splendor of the future!

A future surpassing every philosophy that has ever been spoken.
Thus man can rise above the perfect man.
The history of man proves man to be antiquated and dead;
Thus the synonym of death is man who is the incarnation of it,
And a dealer in the works of it.*

The determining factor of the trust is the scientific realization
Of the apparent, and the balanced equation of the reality.

Is there a purpose?

The purpose of the author of man is to determine in a scientific
Manner whether man can be tempted to think that it is possible
to live
If man can be tempted to think, thereby a better memory can he
create than the one implanted in his mind from the
So-called past.

The implanted memory has been nurtured and kept alive by the
Teachers of the invented memory, who closed their eyes that they
Might not see that the knowledge of the invented memory
Is truly sacred and taboo . . . A forbidden death-dealing tree.

The tree is the three and the three is the ereth or erth: . . . earth.

---

* To here, the 1980 version is identical. For the continuation of the 1980 version, continue on to the next page..

1980 ending of The Invented Memory

The determining factor of the truth
Is the scientific realization of the apparent
And the balanced equation of the reality.

Is there a purpose?

The purpose of the author of man
Is to determine in a scientific manner
Whether man can be tempted to think beyond his own thoughts . . .
Thereby a better memory can be obtained by man
Than the one implanted in his mind from the so-called past.

The implanted memory has been nurtured and kept alive
By the teachers of the invented memory
Who closed their eyes that they might not see
That the knowledge of the invented memory
Is truly sacred and taboo . . .

A forbidden death dealing tree . . . . . The tree is the three,
And the three is the ereth or erth . . . . earth.

Invisibility

Rise lightly from the earth
And try your wings
Try them now
While I make the darkness invisible
The visibility of the day
Is the invisibility of the night
The invisibility of the day
Is the visibility of the night
So rise lightly from the earth
And try your wings
Try them now
While the darkness is invisible.

The Invisible Giants

Fire has many degrees
Brothers of the Flame are like the Fire
For every flame, everywhere and anywhere
Whether large or small
Is a living being
Of the brotherly cosmo-degree of the fire.

The fire is a living being of the non-physical plane
Fire is truly spirit: when it seen, it is still not physical
It is a living breathing being!
For all fire breathes the air
It burns by air.

Out of the wind comes the fire
The fire is the wind
So close are they in spirit
Until each is the spirit of the other.
Twins they are of potent demonstration.
The fire is
And the wind is
Two invisible giants are they.

The Irrisistible Thought

This is the herald of being!
The fiery reality of irrisistible . .
    The living presence
        Of
  The impossible idea.

We will conquer the truths of ignorance
    That we might and will be
    More than just alive . . . .
  But beings of celestial beistness
      Celestial Eternal be am is are on . . . .
    We are the greater: the greater truth
      We are it to be.
  We duplicate ourselves when we choose
We live to bring greater pleasure
And greater delight to the worlds.
    Never will you think we live in vain,
  If you tune your mind to the sound
    Of the sound of the voice
      Of the greater tomorrow.
  Splendidly superb is the future,
Brilliant with the joy of being
      Celestially alive
    Beists of the endless
      Bottomless
      Abyss of the outer never no end endless
        Kingdom of The Eternal ETERNAL BEING.
      The BEIST OF BEISTS . . . .

Jazz In Silhouette

This is the story of the silhouettes,
Bright silhouettes and dark background . . .
Dark silhouettes and bright background.

THIS IS THE SOUND OF SILHOUETTES
IMAGES AND FORCASTS OF TOMORROW
DISGUISED AS JAZZ

There is a velvet sound in the forecast of tomorrow . . .
A velvet sound
Sophisticated, alive and Bold.

MUSIC BY THE SUN AND THE STARS OF TOMORROW . . .
MUSIC BY THE STARS AND THE SUN.
MUSIC: JAZZ IN SILHOUTTES
THIS IS THE MEANING OF THE ALBUM.

A Certain Beat
A Sudden Chord
These things charm the mind with veiled enchantment
That lingers long after the song is done.

IMAGES . . .   VELVET . . .
ENLIGHTMENT . . .   SATURN . . .
HOROSCOPE . . .   HOURS AFTER . . .
BLUES AT MIDNIGHT . . .   ANCIENT AIETHOPIA . . .

These songs are for your memory library
In the artistic form of "JAZZ IN SILHOUTTE"

The Lightning Realities (1972)*

All lights are equally lights
Rays of being
Lightning realities of Vibrations
All lights are
Rays: beams: race
From sound field
To "feel" synchronizes
From rays to race
From race to rays
Through the medium of light
From sundry plane
We move to unlimited
Spheres in unlimited areas:
Areas _____
Transistion weighs
Of abstract translation
To other ways of thought
Equation revealment
The vast abyss: the eternal Pit of Out Space
Is the f[i]rst for bold outcast pioneers
Cast out from the earth into the outer pit

---

* Though there can be no certainty, various textual clues suggest that the composition of this poem may date to the late 1950's.

Lightning Realities (1980)

All lights are rays of being
Lightning realities touch
Intense vibrations . . . . voice of the silences-sound
All lights are of rays . . . beams
Projection from subtle hidden sound field
To feel-synchronization
That moves from rays to race to rays to race to rays
To beams of beings . . . .
Thus, through the medium of light
From sundry cosmo-planes,
We can move to spheres in the vast endless abyss . . . .
The vast endless abyss of Outer Space . . . .
The approach of the Eon of adjustment is at hand
Transition-adjustment . . alter interpretation . . . . . .
Equational-precision
Cosmo-Visions Magic . . . abstract translation
To other waves of thought-feeling-atunement . . .
"The lifting up shall be the casting down",
'Tis thus it is written . . . .
Look outward at the eternal pit of Out-Space . . . .
Out-Space is at first for bold outcast pioneers . . .
Cast Out from the earth into the bottomless pit.

Like Seeds*

They are alike . . . Seeds and words.
When seeds are sown, they become potential
They become potentially active . . . . .
    When words are so-oned
    They become potentially active.
Yes . . . indeed . . . in deed . . .
    Alike they are   . . . .

---

* There appears after this poem on page 60, an untitled poem (found as "Interpretation") which may be a second part of "Like Seeds", but this does not seem likely. There are no other publications of either poem.

Living Parable [1] (1972)

Those who are thirsty for wisdom
Will ever move toward the source of the wisdom
That quenches their thirst.

Living Parallel (1972)

Wisdom on its abstract planes
Uses myth as medium to understanding
Thus a living parable to the outward
or inward truth
Is every myth:
And from the myth you can see
The likeness of the truth-out
Like from a picture
You can see the likeness of a person
And know the person
When first you meet
For the image pictured symbols
Knock upon the door of darkness
And voices speak from without.

Living Parable [2] (1980)

Wisdom on abstract planes
    Uses myth as medium to understanding.
        Thus a living parable to the outward or inward truth
            Is every myth;
                And from the base and crest of the myth
                    You can see like from an all revealing eye
                        The comparison symbol-blueprints of the truth . . . .
                            Like from a picture
                                You can see the likeness of a person
                                    And know the person when first you meet,
                                        For the image pictured symbols
                                            Knock boldly upon the door of darkness
                                                And voices speak from without.

The Lored Lord (1972)*

See the salvation of the Lored
Then you will understand
The meaning of the Lore, the tree of the Lore
See how close the Lore is to the Lored, the Lord.
The Lored should be considered as the Teacher
And if the teacher is the master And the Master is The Lord
The Lore is the knowledge.

*This poem is identical to the poem "The Tree of the Lore" (1980).

Love and Hate

Love which is such a great power must
At times be channeled in a particular
Direction in order to achieve certain intents.
Hate which is such a great power must
At times be channeled in a particular
Direction in order to achieve certain intents.
To lose* one thing above all else is to
Reject the rest or tolerate which is a degree
Of disguised hate in a merciful form.

* While the text reads "lose" here, the correct word may be "love".

Magic City (1972)

This city is the Universe
Because it is that city of all natural creation
It is surrounded by the wilderness
The encircling forest of the edge of itself
All that is endlessly beyond
This city is the Magi's thought
This city is the magic of the Magi's thought.
The idea, the calculated knowledge of it
Eternally balanced by the uncalculated presence of
The intuition potential intruder/the beam
Harmonic precision celestial being
Chromatic rays race.

There are angels.
There are angels!
They guard and watch
Permit and limit . .   . . either way, they are
Powers, principalities and thrones.
They dwell within as well as without the city.

The third heaven slaves?
Who, and what and why are they?
I see places of disguise
Hidden monarchs of the past hid them
The Magi appears as one of them
But they are not
And He the Master Magi is Not!

I see places of disguise
The humanitarians are the Cosmo-cursed oathed of
The Living-God's second-born, they are not the first-born.
And all of this is thus
For someone wrote these words
The second child shall stand in his stead.

Continues on Next Page

Magic City (1972) Continued

The heavens are like a scroll
Blended with circle surrounding earth
And what do we see
Behold!. Behold!.
The stars are writing of the destiny
Of those within the hand of fate
That teacher! That Majesty! That pristine deceiver!
That Magi of belittled/bediminished fame!
That Magi.
For the Magi is miracle Magic of it all
The Magi is all
The All-Magic citizen of the Magic City
Of the Magic universe.

Magic City (1980)

This city is the universe
Because it is that city of all natural creation.
It is surrounded by the wilderness
----- The encircling forest of the edge of itself -----
All that is endlessly beyond this city
   Is the Magi's thought . . . .
      The idea . . . The calculated knowledge of it
        Eternally balanced by the uncalculated presence of
       The potentials' intuition intruder . . . . .
         Projections of harmonic precision
           Cosmo-Omni-rhythms of overtones subtones
           Contrapuntal melodies
            Balanced by ever watchful celestial Feels . .
          They are angels
            They guard and watch . . . permit and limit
           They are powers . . . .
                  Principalities . . . .
                    And thrones . . . .
           They dwell within
 . . . .   As well as without the city . . . . .
The third heaven slaves ? . . . Who and what are they ?
 . . . . I see places of disguise
          Arch-monarchs of the past hid them . .
       The Magi appears as one of them
       For they are not . . . . . .
     And He . . . . The Master Magi is Not !
The heavens are like a scroll
    Blended with circle surrounding earth . . . . .
    And what do we see . . . . . Behold! . . . . Behold!
    The stars are writing of the destiny
     Of those within the hand of fate . . . . .
That Teacher! That Majesty! That pristine Deceiver!
That Magi of belittled/bediminished fame! That Magi!
For the Magi is miracle Magic of it all
The Magi is All . . . .
    The ALL MAGIC CITIZEN of The Magic City
        Of the Magic Universe.

The Mask

I'm working under a mask
There are some of another masque
Where the sun strikes the towers
Beyond the mosque
There is hidden beauty everywhere
And the potentials
Leap across
The barriers of time
Into the
Eternal spirals
Of the
Celestial-Cosmos-lore-way
Beyond the words
Of what is called "life"
And what is called "death".

I'm working under a compelled determination
On a sundry plane
Of
Duplicity-parable-paradox
Where the sun strives
With the ignorance of masses
And the difficulties of tongues
Yet, indeed will achieve
Invincible stance
Bringing all into the dark-cosmo-light
Of a sudden burning celestial-fire . . .

The Melody Of The Air

(from Immeasurable Equation Vol. II, 1972)

This is not to convert
To lead, to persuade
It is of the spirit of the wind.
And what does the wind know?
It never tells.
Where does it go?
It never tells.
Either of the where of, to, or fro
Nor do I.
If everyone is of this planet
Why must they disagree as they do?
The wind wends it's way ever is and on
Trails of clouds sail a path airborne
By the spirit of the wind.
The wind/air/melody/sound
Is
The spirit is air
You need wings to ride
To fly
With the spirit of the air.
The air is melody
Music
That those who feel
Might feel and hear the expressions
Of the feeling
Of the sound
Of the adventure
Of the Living Spirit.

[The Melody of the Air]

(Space is the Place LP Jacket- 1972)

This is not to convert to lead, to persuade
And what does the wind know?
It is of the spirit of the wind
It never tells
Where does it go?
It never tells either of the where of to or from
Nor do I
The wind wends it's way . . . ever is and on
If everyone is of this planet why must they disagree as they
do?
Trails of clouds sail have passed air borne
By the spirit of the wind
The wind-air-melody--sound is
The spirit is air
You need wings to ride to fly with the spirit of the air!

Memory Says (1972)

Quickly, inside the door;
  Greet you, depart:
That's how memory seems-----
Years have no meaning
        (minutes and hours
            and days and years, all the same)
There is no time in memory's realm.
Yesterday?
Last year?
When did I see you last?
OH, I know:
Quickly, inside the door
Greet you, depart . . . . . .
That's what memory says for days and hours.

Memory Says (1980)

Quickly, inside the door;
  Greet you, depart:
    That's how memory seems . . . .
        Years have no meaning
            Minutes and hours
            Days and years,
            All the same . . . . . .
    There is no time in memory's realm.
            Yesterday?
            Last year?
    When did I see you last
        Oh, I know:
            Quickly, inside the door
            Greet you,
                Goodbye . . . . . .
That's what memory says for days and hours.

Men and Amen

What are brothers and what are men
Men is significantly an Egyptian word
For "Egyptians are men and not god."
What are the gods that are not gods
For the gods that are gods
Are perhaps god's gods or God's gods.
God's God's and God's god or God's God
Is mentioned
Assumption?
Idea
Conecption
Idea Knowledge.

Message To Black Youth (1971)

Never say you are unloved
I love you
In all the simplicity of the word
Never say you have no friend
How dare you feel that way!
I am your unknown friend
How long before you know
If I deny you
It is only love
Seeking a way to make you hear
The thought essence of being

It is too late not to be your better self
Your beauty to me is your discipline
If you do not need it now
You will need it then
If you do not need it here
You will need it there

Do you find these strange words for love
Indeed!
I do too
But love is some other truth opposed
Here
If I deny yet I care
No one could ever care more
Than I
Still you may not understand.
But do you must!
Consider this
Well I am jealous then
And why

But it is always why and why and why
That mystery
You are not supposed to know
But I told you yes
Then I told you know*
The vice/voice of the other realm

Outerness there
Listen . . . listen to this
Never say you dwell alone
And think you walk unseen in the darkness
Of the dark black blue** golden brown of you
Here Am I companion friend
Black youth, please understand!

Other youth take heed
prepare
discipline-precision
You will see an abstract tomorrowness myth
A triumph of otherness love
Not the earth definition of . . . . But then
What does the earth know about such things?
Still you shall claim it too
It is great enough for that and more
Not at first meant to be that way
But second thoughts bring other thoughts
Into mind reality/myth
Other youths if real in the myth shall partake.

* The version in the IE Vol.I (1972) has this word as "no".
** The 1972 version has "hue" instead of "blue".

The Mirror of Things To Be (1972)

Henceward and gaze into the mirror of things to be
For that which an ear may hear
The mind's eye can see
Remember this and grasp the helm of boundless intuition-thought
Bypass the snares and traps of the Amen - inner - void
Bypass the snares and traps of the gravity-inner void . . . . .
Remember this:
Someone must show the way
A better way than any other way that they have ever known
Someone must love them more
Than they have ever been loved before
Someone must teach a transformation to a greater truth
Another way of Living-Life ... another ecstacy . . . .
Remember this:
Someone must show the way.

The Mirror of Things To Be (1980)

Henceward and gaze into the mirror of things to be
    For that which an ear may hear,
    The mind's eye can see.
Remember this and grasp the helm
    And grasp the helm of boundless intuition-thought . . . . .
Bypass the snares and traps of the gravity-inner void . . .

Remember this:
    Someone must show the way;
        A better way
            Than any-every other way they have known.

Someone must love them more
    Than they have ever been loved before
        Someone must teach a transformation to a greater truth
            Another way of Living-Being-Ecstacy . . . .
                Remember this:
                Someone must show the way.

Music Of The Spheres

Music of the spheres: of the outer spheres
For there are dimensions
That are, yet are not
This music is of the outer spheres
Of the Kingdom of Not . . . the void
For it is of the unsaid words
Concerning the things that always are to be,
So that from the unsaid words,
Which are of not . . . . .
Because they are of those things
Which always are to be . . . . .
Nothing comes to be in order that
Nothing shall be because nothing
From nothing leaves nothing.

Music of the spheres
This music is of the spheres
Music of the outer spheres
This music came from nothing,
The void, in response to the
Burning need for nothing else
For nothing else will do
For something elseness.
This nothing, this outer void, this outer nothing
Is out of nothing
It is the music of the outer spheres.
The nothing symbol: sphere: nothing is
The earth nothing is 0.
The greater nothing is the endless sphere.

The Myth of Me

Kindness in a cruel world?
What price the glory!
What else is kindness but glory
In a cruel world?
Many words spoken and activated
Activated and spoken in many ways
Are priceless scenarios.
What more could they be than that?
Remote upon the scene
I find the time to realize
That what I find to be
I be and that is all I own --
The thought of the me I wish to be
For nothing else is half as real
As the myth of me.

The Name Sound (1972, version 1)

The name can be music
Played by infinite instruments
The name can lift nothingness
From nothing to reality
And keep the myth parable apparent.

Like once silent voices burst into song
The name strikes the ear
And the sound of it
Rushes like a wild thing
To take its place
As the core
Of the music, the infinite instruments
And the vital vibration
Of the meaning
Of the name

The Name Sound (1972, version 2)

The name can be music played by infinite instruments,
The name can lift splendor-vision from nothing on to
reality-myth
It is the myth of everything that is nothing
It is the nothing that never knew that
was of onceness bounds

Like once silent voices burst into song
The name strikes the ear
And the sound of it
Rushes like a wild thing
To take its place as the core
of the music, the infinite instruments
And the vital realness of the meaning
of the name.

The Name Sound (1980)

The name can be music
Played by infinite instruments.
The name can lift nothingness from nothing
To everluted reality
Yet
Keep the myth-parable apparent.
Like once silent voices burst into song
The name strikes the ear
And
The sound of it
Rushes like a wild thing
To take its place
As the core of the music
The infinite instruments
And the vital vibrations
Of the meaning of the name . . . .

Nature's Laws (IE Vol. I)

According to nature's laws and laws
I be as I am and what I am not even
Because and yet not even because
Because, for, and, that is . . . . why . . . .
Because should and why. If then
Then and so
Perhaps
May
If I do, I will
And if I don't I won't
Either way I do and I don't perspectively
Why, when, how, what, which
Yes, no, neither.

[Nature's Laws]

(Space is the Place LP jacket, 1972)

According to nature's laws and law
  I be as I am and what I am not even
Because and yet not even because
Because and yet not even because
 Because, for, and, that is … why …
Then and so
Perhaps
May
If I do I will
And if I don't I won't
Either way I do and I don't perspectively
Why, when how, what, which
Yes, no . . . . . neither.

The Neglected Plane of Wisdom

Music is a plane of wisdom, because music is a universal
language, it is a language of honor, it is a noble precept, a gift
of the Airy Kingdom, music is air, a universal existence . . .
common to all the living.

Music is existence, the key to the universal language.
Because it is the universal language.
Freedom of Speech is Freedom of Music.
Music is not material, Music is Spiritual.
Music is a living soul force.
That which is of the soul is the greater light
The light of greater instruction . . .
The light of culture and beauty
The light of intensity and living power.
The name of Music is Art.
The name of Music is played by infinite instruments.
The name can lift dreams from nothing to reality . . .
And keep them ever before the eyes . . .
Like once silent voices burst into song, the name strikes the ear
And the sound of it rushes like a wild thing and takes its place as
the core of even the minutest part of being.

Music has wings, it moves upon the wings of intuition and
thought.
Music is the Ambassador of the Airy Kingdom.
Sound . . . Cosmic Vibration . . . Life
Pure life like pure blood is negative.
It is time to consider the negative plane of existence. It is time
to consider Music as a plane of wisdom and a weapon of defense
against the past and the condemnations of the past.

Blood when negative is pure.
The negative is the symbol of the pure.
The Music of the past is positive Music in the same way the past is
symbolized by the positive.

Music The Neglected Plane of Wisdom

Music is a plane of wisdom, because music is a universal language. It is a language of honor, it is a noble precept, a gift of the Airy Kingdom. Music is air, a universal existence . . . common to all the living.

Music is existence, the key to the universal language.
Because it is the universal language . . . .
Freedom of Speech is Freedom of Music.
Music is not material, Music is Spiritual.
Music is a living soul force.
That which is of the soul is the greater light
The light of greater instruction . . .
The light of culture and beauty,
The light of intensity and living power.
The name of Music is Art.
The name of Music is played by infinite instruments.
The name can lift dreams from nothing to reality . . .
    Keeping them ever before the eyes . . .

Like once silent voices burst into song, the name strikes the ear

And the sound of it rushes like a wild thing and takes its place as the core of even the minutest part of being.

Music has wings. It moves upon the wings of intuition and thought.
Music is the Ambassador of the Airy Kingdom.
Sound . . . Cosmic Vibration . . . Life
Pure life like pure blood is negative.
It is time to consider the negative planes of existence.
It is time to consider Music as a plane of wisdom

and a weapon of defense against the past and the condemnations of the past.

Blood when negative is pure.
The negative is the symbol of the pure.
The Music of the past is positive Music in the same way the past is symbolized by the positive.

Note on The Neglected Plane of Wisdom and Music The Neglected Plane of Wisdom

This poem first appeared (as "The Neglected . . .") in the first Saturn records prospectus, issued in 1966 or perhaps 1965. It also appeared in the second Saturn catalog (Saturn "II" Inc. Handy Catalog No. B7S66Y) as "Music The Neglected Plane of Wisdom". The differences between the two are slight, mostly involving punctuation. Both versions are given here because of their great rarity.

At the bottom of "Music The Neglected . . ." is printed "Registered 1955". However, and not surprisingly, no such poem is registered for copyright under either title, or under any of Sun Ra's various names which he used to copyright music. It is not clear then which is the original title or version. If the date is correct, this poem is the earliest known Sun Ra poem.

Never is the Future (1972)

Never is the future

Because Tomorrow never comes
        Comes tomorrow never
        Tomorrow comes never
        Comes never tomorrow
        Never comes tomorrow
        Never tomorrow comes.*

           TOMORROW IS NEVER

The future is never
        Never comes tomorrow
        Never is not

Never is not necessarily negative
      There are two nevers
          The name of one is once
             For once is not and never is not

If never is not then ever is ot
If dot is dart, then ever is art
What eternity does the eternity represent?
What cycle of ever is the art?

    Behold the pre-prophetic symbols of the planes of Never.
Behold, behold this thisness!
This isness.

That which is to be will be
But that which will be is not
Thus is to be and will be are not
Yet that which will never be was is the eternal future.

* See also the poem "Tomorrow Never Comes" which is similar to this excerpt.

NEVER IS THE FUTURE . . . . . since if NEVER never was
Or is not of the never that has been
Then the never which is not of the was is the IS.
    The alter future consists of endless nevers
Nevers of motion which continues to be alive and active.
        Consider the motion and the notion
        It takes a motion to notion
        and it takes a notion to motion.

Never Is The Future (1980)

Never is the future
Because tomorrow never comes
        Comes tomorroow never
        Tomorrow comes never
        Comes never tomorrow
        Never comes tomorrpw
        Never tomorrow comes . . . . . .
Tomorrow is never and never is tomorrow
When a planet makes it's home in the shadow of the past,
Coming events will always be the same as those of once . . . .
Once upon a time is the realm of yesterday . . . .
Tomorrow never touches the shores of a world of yesterday . .
Tomorrow never ever comes that way
Yesterday is once and was
Tomorrow is always never been
It is not in the realm of time that passes away . . . .
This potent equation-symbol points the way
To Omni-Immortality.
        Behold the pre-prophetic symbols
        Of the planes of Never
    Behold this This-ness!
        This Is Is-ness.

New Horizons

Music Pulsing like a living heartbeat,
Pleasant intuition of better things to come . . .
The sight of boundless space
Reaching ever outward as if in search of itself.
Music spontaneous rapture,
Feet rushing with the wind on a new world
Of sounds:
Invisible worlds . . . . vibrations . . . tone pictures . . *
A new world for every self
Seeking a better self and a better world.

Music akin to thought . . . .
Imagination . . . !
With wings unhampered,
Unafraid . . . .
Soaring like a bird
Through the threads and fringes of today
Straight to the heart of tomorrow.
Music rushing forth like a fiery law
Loosening the chains that bind,
Ennobling the mind
With all the many greater dimensions
Of a living tomorrow.

* The text to this point was set to music by Arganny Jones as "Tone Pictures", copyrighted in 1957. Jones was presumably an acquaintance of Sun Ra's, since the copyright address is Sun Ra's appartment at the time.

The No End

Only to be bottomless humble
Is to be bottomlessly cast out
Until there is none to compare
Only to be bottomlessly ignorant
Is to be the other state of ecstasy
That ignorance which is of and to the unknown
And this unknown is of the greater chaos . . . .
For chaos is the immeasurable
A design formless as to the idea of form
And of the desire to synchronize to that end
Which is and yet is not the end
Paradox
A synchronization to the infinity . . . . the infinity . . .
The no-end
Cosmic chaos . . . .

The No Point

The vibrations advance to further consideration . . . . .
Consider:
The invisible vibration
Word patterns . . . formula scheme . . . . .
Sagas of concept enact themselves: Conceive:
Give reign to thought potentials.
Out of nowhere they come like embers suddenly aflame
With living reach
Spiral infinity
Being.

Yes, Out of nowhere they come from the no point
Purposeless Cosmanitarian-Guardian-Differentialer
Of the die cast by those who gamble
With
Fate's decisions voice.

------ A whirlpool of sub-mid-over-transient
Tone projections----------------------------

The vibrations ride on the oceans of the air
Where rendezvous myth with dream-reality . . . . . .
At the crossroads of Destiny . . . It is spirit air . . . . . .
The golden silence lingers all around . . . .
It is a festival of soundness
Word duplicity
Like harmonic . . . . enharmonic change
When the person Myth meets the person Reality
The spirit of the impossible-strange appears
In dark disguise
It is always there where nothing inverts itself
And becomes something
Whatever is the imperative need
Yet different nothings activate themselves
To become different somethings . . . .
It is Creations-matrix Diversifier . . . .

Nothing Is

At first nothing is;
Then nothing transforms itself to be air
Sometimes the air transforms itself to be water;
And the water becomes rain and falls to earth;
Then again, the air through friction becomes fire.
So the nothing and the air and the water
And the fire are really the same---
Upon different degrees.

The Observers

Observer I
I observe
The once I was/and the Is I Am
I be and Observe
The are of me.

Observe We
We observe
The once We were/and the Is We Are
We be and observe
The are of We

Of Celestial Cosmo Key*

In this age, the invented memory
>>Will be used
>As an
Outerverted radiation point,
>>Because
>>Inwardly
The invented memory was secret
>>And still is
>To those, who do not wish to learn . . . . .
>>>But
Outwardly, the invented memory
>>Is a
>Celestial Cosmo Key
>To the wisdom
>>Of
>Understanding feeling.
>Life as it is known on planet earth
>>At this time is the synonym of death.
They often walk together hand in hand . . . . . .
It is imperative to understand that the planes
Of existence on planet earth are primary . .
>Placing them both in the balance
>>And leaving the balance as the rest
>>>Is a fitting solution : : : : : : : :
>Solved by bypass intrigue . . . .
Once in the territoty of the non tree
And the non knowledge of the non good
>And the non evil
Adjustments must be made to reach the omni . . .

* The original text is in all capitals.

Of Coordinate Vibrations

Everything is simple
If the coordinate vibrations coincide . . . . . .
Nothing is no,
But no is the inversion of the on.
The sound is of the wind
The wind is not
But the not is the note
And note permutated is tone.
Music is of the epi-cosmic ray point.
It is of mathematical symbolic-permutation.
The epi-cosmic scene can not be seen
By ordinary standard orientation eyes . . . . . .
It is this determination
That reveals it's nature . . . .
A concentration . . . a point of energy
Whence to project, to conceive
To create the nothing of the point.
Music envisions and potentializes,
It limits or extends
It is also of the psychometric endeavor.
The nothing is the whole note of music.
Within that nothing
Is the divisional manifestations
Of the elements of rhythm
And the analyzation quintessence of the melody.
Music is a voice
A differential sound of words.
A grammar and a language
As well as a synthesizer.
It is the reach towards it's twin immortality.

Of Days (1972)

I dream
Of all the days that are not
The never days that belong to me
Of living friends and living home
With laughter round an open hearth

I dream of these
For these days are mine
My treasures beyond compare
They are not and never
But once their image passed me by
And I thought I felt
The touch of happiness
Now I know it was
Only a shadow of the real
Projected to a shadow world
Of images and shadows
That moved with lightnin' speed
Into the eternity
Of that which they call
The beginning
And yet I see beyond that point
For there is counterpoint and counterpoint
      And counterpoint dimensions dimension
It is music like the music . . . .
The music swells to undescribeable sound
     Of mystic Everness Eternal Beingness
        Chromatic Rhythms
        Multi - vision

Of Days (1980)

I dream : The never days that belong to me
  Of living friends and living home
    With laughter 'round an open hearth.

I dream of these
  Of these
    For these days are mine
      My treasures beyond compare . . . .
       Are of not and never;
        But once their image passed me by
         And I thought I felt
        The touch of happiness . . . . . .
          Now I know
         It was only a shadow of the real
         Projected to a shadow world
        Of images and shadows
         That moved with light
          Into the eternity
          Of that which they call
          The beginning.

        Still and yet,
         I see beyond that point . . . . . .
       For there is counterpoint and counterpoint
      And counterpoints sub/overtones dimension
      It is music like the music
       The music swells to undescribeable sound
      Of mystic everness Eternal Beingness
Chromatic multi-vision-melodic-harmonic rhythms.

Of Enforced Reality

Surely by now
The world should see
What they think is true
Is not.
For centuries
The world at large
Has not been able to feel
The difference
Bewtween what is untrue
And what is real.
The history of this enforced 'reality'
Is not celestials will to be . . . .
This realm of escalating hate
Is not the work of pureness-fate.

. . . Of Hidden Tomes*

We speak in hidden tones
Invisible tomes to you
For if you
Fully knew . . . . . .
It is still problematical
As to what
You would will to be or do . . . .

* The original text is in all capitals.

Of Kindred Folks

I am trying to find myself:
Find the idea from which I sprang;
Find the forest whereof I know it lives,
Find the trees whereof I am alike.
There are no roots for trees on city pavements
In blase minds.
Let me find trees like myself
The same height as I
The same kind as I,
That I might raise my limbs in majesty to the sky
The same as they
Trees of kindred spirit
Trees attuned to me,
Whose leaves rustle with music
To the soft accompaniment of the winds.
Trees who do not dwarf me in any way
Hiding the sunlight from my face;
Trees to whom I am not a giant
Unalike, alien, strange
Casting shadows in their way
Trees that are not scrawny
Malcontent
Inclined to ugliness . .
Trees that are themselves
As I am myself;
Trees that I can always call
Mt Living Friends.

[Sins] Of Not When (1980)*

What myth am I?
They? You?
Him
Us . . . . we
What
How
Which
Where
And
That
So
If
Those
Then
Me
Them
Why?
What myth yet
Too
He
It
Her
All
Since
Of
Not
When.

INTERSTELLAR LOW WAYS   203

SUN RA and his MYTH SCIENCE ARKESTRA

FEATURING

SUN RA, Piano
JOHN GILMORE, Tenor
PAT PATRICK, Baritone, Flute
MARSHALL ALLEN, Flute, Alto
RONNIE BOYKINS, Bass
LUCIOUS RANDOLPH, Trumpet
GEORGE HUDSON, Trumpet
EDWARD SKINNER, Percussion
WILLIAM COCHRAN, Percussion

ONWARD George Hudson, Trumpet; John Gilmore, Tenor;
     Sun Ra, Piano.
SOMEWHERE IN SPACE Sun Ra, Piano; John Gilmore, Tenor;
     Marshall Allen, Flute; Ronnie Boykins, Bass.
INTERPLANETARY MUSIC Sun Ra, Piano; Vocal by the Arkestra;
     Ronnie Boykins, Space Gong; Interplay by Sun Ra.
INTERSTELLAR LOW WAYS Sun Ra, Piano; John Gilmore, Tenor;
     Marshall Allen and Pat Patrick, Flute; followed with
     Marshall Allen on Flute; Sun Ra, Piano; William Cochran
     on Drums; Ronnie Boykins, Bass; again Sun Ra, Piano,
     Chimes, Gong; Pat Patrick, Bells and Claves.
SPACE LONELINESS Lucious Randolph, Trumpet; Sun Ra, Piano;
     Marshall Allen, Alto.
SPACE AURA Sun Ra, Piano; George Hudson, Trumpet; John Gilmore,
     Tenor; George Hudson, Trumpet.
ROCKET NUMBER NINE Vocal by the Arkestra; Edward Skinner, Drums;
     Sun Ra, Piano; John Gilmore, Tenor; Ronnie Boykins, Bass;
     Sun Ra, Piano.

"THE IMPOSSIBLE IS THE WATCHWORD OF THE GREATER SPACE AGE"
THE SPACE AGE CANNOT BE AVOIDED AND THE SPACE MUSIC IS THE
KEY TO UNDERSTANDING THE MEANING OF THE IMPOSSIBLE AND EVERY
OTHER ENIGMA.   -- SUN RA

SIDE A

ONWARD
SOMEWHERE IN SPACE
INTERPLANETARY MUSIC
INTERSTELLAR LOW WAYS

SIDE B

SPACE LONELINESS
SPACE AURA
ROCKET NUMBER NINE TAKE OFF FOR PLANET VENUS

* Identical poem "Sins of Not When" published in 1972.

Of Notness

The kingdom of not . . . . .
A realm of myth.
See the mythery
Of the non-existent-mystery . . .
It is not but yet is . . .
It has never been on cosmo--evident-isness
Thus it not of the past
And hence is not of the passed.
Consider the hidden presence of the
Of the kingdom of not . . . .
A realm of angelic-celestial-myth . . . .
And no one knows where
But still it is yet always there . . . . . .

Behold!
   The Celestial enigma
     Of that which is not
    But yet always is Is . . . . . Like to of
        Isis . . . .
          Is IS . . . .

-2-

INTERSTELLAR LOW WAYS

RECORDED   1961   EL SATURN STUDIO   CHICAGO

PUBLISHER: ENTERPLANETARY KONCEPTS, BMI

PRODUCER: ALTON ABRAHAM

Compositions and arrangements by SUN RA

Of The Contemporary Scene '78

First came the songs and scenes of Go-Go-Go
And unrelated strikes galore.
After that came tremendous snow . . . .
The snow of '78
Determined greatly the fate
Of economy
And the shape of things to be.

America kept its date with destiny;
There was no place to hide or flee
Yet and still America's existence
        Is the spiritual mystery.
For although many things of value unnoticed
            Pass by,
Pure and separate from the lie
Of what they call "life"
Which is better called aimless strife
And the treasure-house of wealth
For which they dig is captured--imprisoned death,
Give glory and clap your hands
The miracle of Ameica that it still stands . . . . .
All is not lost!
Some Ameicans have paid the cost . . .
Just a little while and you will see
The key to every mystery . . . .
First comes the alter-destiny music-cosmo-song . . .
Then patterned-roles fall to those
        To whom they belong
  The music issues a call
  It is the omni-answer to it all.

Of The Cosmic Blueprints

If it was not slavery---
It was rather complete service to humanity,
Unstinted humble-effort
Foolishness to the world
But bolder and braver
Than any of history's warriors.

If it was not slavery---
It was the activation
Of the Cosmic-blueprints . . .
Sowing* seeds of cosmos rare
Casting ever down to ever lift above.

If it was not slavery
It was the freedom not to be
In order to ready for the discipline-plane
From other-greater-worlds.

* In the Umbra Anthology (1968), this word is "Showing", which seems incorrect. The Black Fire version and the 1980 version have "Sowing". Also, the Umbra version is the only one with stanzas.

Of The Day That Died

The past always reminds me of the day that died
It shall not come again
Because it dwells in the realm of "been"
And that which has been
Is forever separated from that
Which is to be.

Of The Myth

Of the myth am I
The name and voice of the outer void.
From the outer nothing
Beyond the enclosed circle of the third heaven
The third heaven: the planet earth
The world deed/act
The world called earth.

Of The Planet Earth

Gamma . . . Gimel . . . Ge   . . . .
Planet earth is the planet three
Gamma . . . . Gimel . . . . . Ge
See the graphs of geography
Gamma . . . Gimel . . . Ge
Don't forget geology.
Gamma . . Gimel . . . . Ge
Observe the word tree trinity
The Godhead trio-three
Gamma . . . Gimel . . . Ge
The third planet . . planet three
Alpha-Beta unity
A + B = 3
AB the father . . . Hebrew see?
AB the father # 3
Earth and heaven mystery!

Gamma . . . Gamma . . . . . . Gimel . . . Ge
Cursed with guilt where none should be
Gamma . . . Gimel . . . . Gamma . . Ge . . . . .
Though one, the earth's still planet three.
Permutation of the three . . . . .
Earth is erth . . . you plainly see.
Revelation mystery!
Saga deep of planet three!
. . . . . . Gamma . . Gamma . . . Gimel . . . . Gee!!!!!!
Ab the orb . . . octaveity
Bro to bar infinity . . . .

Of The Pattern Of Being

I laid on earth
Pressed my face to the ground
And felt the pulse of it.
Arose strong!   . . . .

Strong!!!
From the magnetism of its strength.
Arose and walked away
With head high
And shoulders proud . . .
Proud to have dreamed my dream;
Proud to have pressed myself
To the broad solid earth . . . .
Alive with living . . . . . .
Alive with dreams
Alive with all
Attuned to the song of living
Alive with all
That is weaved into the pattern
Of Being.

Of Variable Universe (1972)

When one is primary - young
All the ideas in the world
Converge in counsel
And through disguised declarations
Play upon one's brain
Like fringes upon some tender instrument
Impressionable days of splendor
Electric - naturalness
Flash lightning - touch
Upon the time - negatives
Of variable universe
And one feels is not what words express:
The never-plane, the alter-ever-on-out
Inexpressible Infinity

Of Variable Universe (1980)

When one is primary-young,
All the ideas in the world converge in counsel
And through disguised declarations
Play upon one's brain
Like upon fringes of some tender instrument . . . . . .
Those years are impressionable ever-days
Of treasure-splendor
Unfettered . . . unknowing innocence

When one is primary-young
Feelings touch like flash-lightning's play
Upon the time negatives of variable universe
Time negatives of variable universe
Negatives of variable univeres
Of variable universe
Omni . . . . . alter ever on
Inexpressible OMNI-INFINITY . . . .
OMNI INFINITY . . . .

"Omniverse"

Omniverse-
Is
The totality
Of
All the universes
And you
Are welcome
To
Be citizens
Of
The Omniverse

On (1972)

The Spaceward will take you spacewise/spaceward
A tree to make one wiseward
    Wise/ward
        Y's YH's YHST
        Wordward*   wordward
            Alpha/omega
Wardword
    Word ward
        [ward word]**
    inward
        in ward
            outward
                out ward
                    space
                        Void

A tree to make one wise/wist/wihst
        The spacewise will take you spaceward
        Space word
        Space
        Nothing
         infinity
            Ever outward
                On and On and On
                Ontology
                On
                    On and On, and On and On
                        Father/Farther+
                On
                    Farther
                        Farther
                            Farther On.

* This word is ommitted in the 1980 version.
** This line is in the 1980 version but not the 1972 version.
+ This line is not in the 1980 version.

On Solar Planes

New sounds cause new vibrations
Like ripples on a lake
They branch out from the propulsion
Point of activation.
New sounds!
New sound crash the shield of illusion-hypnosis
And one can plainly see
That the 'life' of the world
Is only the manifestation
Of a particular interpretation.

In the same way
The world is what it is
The way shall be what the
World is to be
All the seeds of all
Can be assuaged by the equation!
The solar planes
Are the solar planes
Thence fly the solar ones
On solar planes to solar planes.

On The Bypass

On the bypass
The narrow way
Above the late earth*
Planes of comprehension
Bypast the cycle of former things.
On the bypass
Of the spiral way
The spiral trascends
The misinterpreted things of sin.

* In the 1980 version, this word is capitalized and in quotes.

On The Edge of the Thin-Between (1972)

Suddenly I awake from sleep
Footsteps pattering on the rim
On the edge of the thin between
I rush to the window
Look down into the streets below
Look out into space
Look fearfully behind me
But there is nothing
I see nothing anywhere
There is no sound
Only the echoes
Of that which awoke me
Footsteps pattering on the rim
On the edge of the thin between.

On The Edge Of The Thin Between (1980)

Suddenly I awake from sleep
Footsteps pattering
On the rim . . . . . .
On the edge of the thin between.
 . . . . .I rush to the window
 . . . . . .Look down into the streets below
 . . . . Look out into space . . . .
 . . . . . Look fearfully behind me . . . .
But there is nothing; . . . .
No sign of what I heard . . . .
There is no sound . . . .
Except . . . only the echoes of that which awakened me
Footsteps pattering on the rim
On the edge of the thin between.

Once Upon A Time (1980)*

Let the centuries be your enlightment
Read your histories
Your history of oneness
Your history of once upon a time
Once upon a time
But before once was nothing
And after once is twice
Never before the once
And twice the presence of never
The pleasant nothing of never
For nothing
Nothing is
And nothing from nothing leaves
Nothing
And one from one leaves
Nothing
And two from two leaves nothing
And three from three leaves nothing
And everything from everything leaves nothing
And nothing from nothing inverted leaves
Everything
So if one sends one
There is nothing
For one from one
Leaves nothing
There is nothing in the never land
Of Never.

* This poem is identical to the last part of "Circle Eternity" (1972). See page 8-9.

The Order of the Ardor (1972)

The vibrations of the ardor and the order
Are so convincingly alike
Only pure instinct
Can intuite the fine distinction
What is the order of the ardor,
And what is the ardor play
Which symbolizes
The way and the weigh of the order.

A new ardor
Can *foundate* a new order
As the end
Because the ardor is
The first thought thrust into being.

The Order Of The Ardor (1980)

The vibrations of the ardor and the order
Are so convincingly alike
Only pure instinct can intuite the fine distinction
Between the order of the ardor
And the ardor of the order . . . .
The enigma of the Passion play
Which symbolizes the way of the weigh
And the weigh of the way:
Which is the law of the order.
And the ardor of the law and order
On psychic planes of revelation
Concerning the why
Of the why
Things are the way they are.
A different order can *foundate* a different ardor
A different ardor/passion/desire/aim/end
Is necessary to make life harmonious
Sympathetic and beautiful Cosmo-Real.

Other Gods Have I Heard Of (1972)

For you
I gave up every thing I never had
For all I never had is the "life" I abandoned
I gave up everything I never had
All my pleasant fancies and dreams
Which concerned only me
All that earth would call a good life
I gave up all this for you
Because my love for you
Is greater than all the worlds
And more immeasurable than the universe
Greater love has no man.

And Greater love has no god than I
For I like my greater love
Am immeasurable
And my words are more than life
And more than death
What else am I than the greater
Myth of all myths.

Other gods have I heard of
But they were not as I
Other gods people have I seen
Accordingly
But they are not as mine.
Other people* gods have I heard of
But they are not as the gods I know.

* Should be, perhaps "peoples'" as in the revision.

Other Gods Have I Heard Of (1980)

For you
I gave up everything I never had;
For all I never had is the life of the life I abandoned
Yes, I gave up everything I never had: --------------
All my pleasant fancies and dreams
Which concerned only me.
All that earth would call a good life,
I bypassed . . . . I gave up all this for you.
And who is the you, I love so dearly?
Ye pure in heart, It is ye
My love for you is greater than all the worlds
And more in height and depth than the universe.
Greater love has no god than I
For I like my greater love am of the immeasurable . . . .
And my words are more than life
And more than death . . . .
What else am I than the Myth-Impossibility
Yes . . . Other gods have I heard of
But they were not as I . . . .
Other gods people have I seen,
Accordingly . . . .
But they are not as mine.
Other peoples gods have I heard of
But they are not like my Eternal Friend
The Omni-Master GOD and his celestial court of Angel gods.

The Other Otherness (1972)

When one understands
There is no ego involved
There is no communication
In the supervised state of distances
For we who are
Know we are to is
To be
To rise above an evoluted eternity
To feel our worthless pricelessness
Invaluable similitude
A separate only onliness
Only on
Movement out to behold kindred outerness
An other-otherness
That is not like them
If they are of a non-similarity vibration

The Other Otherness (1980 - version 1)

When one understands
There is no ego involved
When speaks true feelings reach sypathetic touch
Even the farflung worlds of Heaven listens in delight.
For we who are intuitively aware
Know we are to be
To rise above the earth's tomorrowless eternity . . . . .
To feel our worthless pricelessness
Rare similitude . . . .
On-liness
Only On
Movement out to behold kindred othernesses
Of and from other worlds
beyond worlds . . . .
    Beyond worlds . . . . beyond worlds beyond worlds . . . .

The Other Otherness (1980 - version 2)

When one understands through feeling
There is no gravity geo-captivity
Communication-point
Through the earth-ego-involvement desire.
Thus the supervised state of distances,
And earth-bound limitations
Are no longer valid.
The celestial spirit master dwells
Above and within . . . .
For we who are know we are to is . . .
To be and am
We be am
To beam-synchronize
Within its energy-rays . . . .
To rise above
The
Revoluted-eternity . . . . . .
To feel our worthless pricelessness
Invaluable rare celestial touch
To reach
A separate onliness to own and on.
The onness movement out
To behold kindred otherness
Cosmo-mysteries
Of an other otherness
That is not like to or of
Their themness
If they are of a non-similarity
Vibration-intensity.

Other Planes Of There (1966)

The displaced years
Memory calls them that
They were never were then;
Memory scans the void
And from the future
Comes the wave of the greater void
A pulsating vibration
Sound span . . . . . . bridge to other ways and
Other planes of there . . . .

Other Planes Of There (1972)

The displaced years
Memory calls them that
They were never were then;
Memory scans the void
And from the future
Comes the wave of the greater void
[A]* pulsating vibration
Sound bridge and span
To other ways
And other planes
Of there.

* This word
is in the
Immeasurable
Equation
Volume II
version but not
in Volume I.

Other Planes Of There (1980)

The displaced years
   Memory calls them that.
      They were never was then . . . .
    Memory scans the void
     And from the future
      Comes the wave of the greater void
    A pulsating vibration
     A sound span and bridge
    To other ways
       other planes of there.

The Other Side Of Music (1972)

Some music is of specialized interpretation.
Some music is of synchronization precision.
Every light is a vibrational sight and sound:
It is rhythm in harmony with beam/rays/intensification
and projection visibility.
Music is light and darkness . . . precedent
of vitality . . . stimulation extraordinary
Equational harmonic differential pause prelude
to the sound that is on its way . . .
EVERY PLACE THERE IS, IS MUSIC. CHAOS
IS MUSIC AND HARMONIOUS PEACE IS MUSIC
What direction does it: decides the way until . . .

Silence is music.
There are different kinds of silences:
each silence is
A world all its own.
In a lesser but not least important sense,
Silence is an integral part of all music:
in a fractional sense,
When judged metrically.

We must not forget transposition.
Transposition always results in a
change of color.
Behold the vastness of music,
It is as vast as the greater allness
and the greater neverness . . .
And too music in its meta-phases
must not be ignored.

Are you thinking of metaphysics
alone? Well, don't.
In the future (and even as of Now),
you will have to contend with and
recognize METAMENTAL and METASPIRIT:
also you will come face to face with
oblique METATHESIS.

The Other Side Of Music (1980)

Some music is of specialized interpretation;
Some music is of synchronization precision
Every light is a vibrational sight and sound . . .
And every dark is a vibrational sight and sound . .
It is rhythm in harmony with beam/rays
Intensification and projection visibility . . . .

Music is lightness and darkness
Precedent of vitality . . . stimulation extraordinary
Stimulation extraordinary . . . .
Equational harmonic differential pause prelude
Prelude to the sound that is on its way . . . . .

Every place there is . . . there is music . . . .
Chaos is music and celestial harmonius
And celestial harmonius peace is music . . . .
What direction does it: decides the way until . . .

Silence is music too . . . .
There are different kinds of silences . . . .
Each silence is a world all its own
Thus:

> In a lesser but not least important sense,
> Silence is an integral part of all music . . .
> When thought of in the micro-fractional way.

We must not forget transposition.
Transposition always
Is a change of color.
Behold the vastness of music
> It is the greater allness approach . . .

Other Thoughts (1972)

Now and then I pause
From the hectic pace
This timeless role
Now and then
. . And scan the faces that I see
. . . Look in the eyes of them
. . . . Searching for the common touch
. . . . . The anti-oath-like bonds
. . . . . . The other parts of me.

Now and then tiring of what they call reality
Bruised and beaten by its force
I step into the friendly city of the forest
Of what they call illusion
There to tend my wounds
And heal them
With the light nin'* touch
Of balanced thought
And the splendid comradeship of other worlds . . . . .

* Given as " lightnin' " in all subsequent versions.

The Outer Beyond

Without from the outer-beyond
Comes the yearning
An un-named desire
Intense, persistent desireless desire . . .
A space whirlpool of wisdom-sounds
Intensifying the point to which I activate . . .
Within from without
Comes lightning - like
A fire-rain of thoughts . . . .

Rare sentiment
And untouched feeling of images . . . . . .
Abstract images of another time
Another time yet to be
Of Cosmo-deep infinity
Omni-alter-outer way
Is the password for today.

The Outer Bridge (1965)

In the half-between world
Dwell they the tone-scientists
Sound
Mathematically precise
They speak of many things
The sound-scientists
Architects of planes of discipline

The Outer Bridge (1972)

In the half-between world
Dwell they, the sound-scientists
Mathematically precise . . . . . .
They speak of many things
The tone scientists
Architects of planes of discipline.

The Outer Bridge (1980)

In the half-between world,
Dwell they: The tone scientists . . . .
In notes and tone
They speak of many things . . . .
The tone scientists:
Architects of planes of discipline.
Mathematically precise are they:
The tone-scientists.

The Outer Darkness (1972 - version 1)

Black is space: THE OUTER DARKNESS
the void direction to the heavens.
Each spaceport planet is a heaven/haven.
Planet earth is erth (permutation
thre/three), (it is a planet #3 from the sun)
From this reckoning is* is the third heaven.
The music of the outer darkness is
the music of the void.
The opening is the void: but the
opening is synonym to the
beginning.
This is an indication interpretation.
. . . Some music is of specialized
interpretation . . .
. . . Some music is of synchronization
precision . . . . . .
Sometimes music becomes more than
music. And this thought reach
is of the incredible plane.

---

* In 1980b this text is corrected to read "From this reckoning/Planet earth is the third heaven."

The Outer Darkness (1972 - version 2)

Intergalactic music is of the Outer Darkness
Therefore it is of the greater Blackness
And from that point of view
It is Black Infinity
And from that point of view
It is Natural Black Music.
. . . It is the music of Natural-Black Infinty . . . .
It is unlimited in scope
Immeasurable in it's multiplicities and potentialities.
Natural Black music projects the myth of Blackness
And he who is not Black in spirit will never know
That these words are true and valid forever.
I speak of different kind of Blackness, the kind
That the world does not know, the kind that the world
Will never understand
It is rhythm against rhythm in kind dispersion
It is harmony against harmony in endless coordination
It is melody against melody in vital enlightenment
And something else and more
A living spirit gives a quickening thought.

The Outer Darkness (1980)

Intergalactic music is of the outer darkness
Therefore it is of the greater Void-Blackness
And from that point of view:
. . . . It is Black-Infinity:
. . . . And from that point of view:
. . . . It is Cosmo-Nature's music . . . . . .
. . . . It is the music of natural-spontaneous Infinty
. . . . It is unlimited in scope . . . .
Immeasurable in its multiplicities and potentialities.
Natural dark-black music projects the myth of ever Is
And he who is not dark in spirit will never know
That these words are true and valid forever.
I speak of different kind of blackness,
The kind that the world does not know . . . .
The kind that the world will never understand.
. . . . . . It is rhythm against rhythm in kind dispersion,
. . . . . . It is harmony against harmony in endless coordinate
. . . . . . It is melody against melody in dark-enlightenment
. . . . . . It is Nature's voice in Cosmo-Sound
. . . . . . It is the everything and the subtle nothing
            Of Omni-All
. . . . . It is the ever quickening-presence of The Living Spirit
. . . It is the Cosmo-bridge to the Dark Unknown Eternal.

Parallels (1970)

If it is not here
It must be there
For somewhere and nowhere
      Parallels
In versions of each other . . . . where
Or even before something came to be

Parallels (1972)

If it is not here
It must be there
For somewhere and nowhere
Parallels
In versions of each other
Where/when nothing after something is not
Or even before something came to be.

Parallels (1980)

If it is not here,
It must be there:
For somewhere and nowhere parallels
In secret versions of each other's where
Or even before somethings came to be.

The Past is a Dream (1972)

The past is a dream
A fictitious fantasy devised
By some sardonic kindly mind
In the hope that we might see
The meanings of today and all it's possibilities
And that in our gratitude
We would not live in such a way
That we should retrogress
To all the mean lowliness
Of our imagined yesterdays.
The past is some ficticious thing
A one dimension fantasy
Made to be or seem to be . . . . In the hope that we might see
Beyond the scene of shadow-past
Yes to see, we must to see
The Living beauty sympathy,
The greater Alter-universe
Is just the place where we should be.
This present dream is not the thing
This dream we will that it not be
This one dimension fantasy.

The Past Is Like A Dream (1980)

The past is like a dream . . . .
A fictitious fantasy devised
By some sardonic kindly mind . . . .
In the hope that we might see
The meanings of today and all it's possibilities;
And that in our gratitude,
We would not live in such a way
That we should retrogress
To all the mean lowliness
Of our imagined yesteryears.
The past is a fabrication-thing
Some fictitious one-dimension fantasy . . . .
Made to be or seemed to be real,
In the hope that we might see
With intuition vision's-eye
Beyond the shadow scenes of yesterdays.
Yes to see . . . . we must to see
The living beauty sympathy . . . .
. . . . The greater Alter-Universe is just the place
Where we should be . . . .
This earth-bound dream
Is illusions child . . . .
A strong delusion
A one-dimension fantasy.

The Pivoting Planes (1972)

When the word was spoken,
IT WAS BALANCED ON THE
        PIVOTING PLANES OF SOUND,
When it was written, it reflected one plane of sight
      And the triple meaning with its multi-divisions
Was no longer apparent,
       Because the meaning of the balanced word
     on the PIVOTING PLANES
              cannot be written as revealingly as it
               can be thought of and felt
       Because the idea of the PIVOTING PLANES
        is like a touch of vibrating magic
          And the magic is the wisdom-ignorance
         Of unspeakable understanding
         intuition.
Thus   is   the   idea   of the PIVOTING PLANES
      of the
    greater impossible
      and the
   Imeasureable
       equation
    SPACE-VOID
      reality
      on
      the
      outer reach
       of the unending
       On
        ONNESS "O   N."

The Pivoting Planes Of Sound (1980)

When the word was spoken,
It was balanced on the pivoting planes of sound . . . .
When it was written,
It reflected one plane of sight.
Thus the triple meaning with it's multi-divisions
      was no longer apparent;
         Because
The meaning of the balanced word
  On the pivoting planes
    Cannot be written as revealingly
   As it can be
     thought of and felt
     Because
    The idea of the pivoting planes
  Is like the touch of vibrating magic
And the magic is the wisdom-ignorance
Of unspeakable understanding intuition . . . .
Thus is the idea of the pivoting planes
  Of the greater impossible and the equation-enigma
   Reality-Void.

The Place of the Searching I

Wherever they are going
I will not go there
Whatever they are being
I will not be where
I seek the beist reach
The place of the searching I
There is nothing more to anything but nothing
There is nothing more to nothing but anything
Everywhere and everything
Anything and nothing.

The Plane: Earth (1968)

Every planet is a small plane
In the universe
Planet means
Small plane
When considered
According to a certain standard

Every plane is a plane* T
Planet three is Plane T three
T, then, is a symbol for the plane earth.

---

* In Omni Press versions of this poem, this word is given as "plan", which is probably a misprint.

Planes Of Nature (1972)

If they would rise above their wisdom
They could see nature as it is
And they would understand
That there are planes of nature
Greater than the plane they know.
All around them
Are the other measure
To the other wisdom-ignorance-myth.

Planes Of Nature (1980)

If they would rise up above their knowledge
They would be able to see with their intuition's-heart
They would be able to see beyond their sight
Their spirit's eye could pierce the night
Where earth dwells in hooded shame
Yes, earth was once a noble name.
If they would rise up above their yes-bound self
They would know the things to no . . . .
Then they would see nature as it is
And at long last they would feel
The touch of Cosmo-Real
And they would know that they know they know
That there is no need to know,
If you cannot feel.

Point

There is a point
Where nothing is everything
Where everything is seemingly nothing
On a diminished plane
That is the point.
I saw the point
Where I could not accept
The world
And I could not accept
It
I saw the point
Where I stood
At the crossroads
Of the world of words
The point
Where I stood astonished at the moving distance
Of destiny
And I determined a determination-potential.

Points On The Space Age (1957)

This is the music of greater transition
To the invisible irresistible space age.
The music of the past will be just as tiny in the world of the
future
As earth itself is in the vast reach of outer space.
Outer space is big and real and compelling
And the music which represents it must be likewise.
The music of the future is already developed
But the minds of the people of earth must be prepared to accept it.
The isolated earth age is finished
And all the music which represents only the past
Is for museums of the past and not for
The moving panorama of the outer spacite program.

Points Of The Space Age (1984)*

THE SPACE AGE CANNOT BE AVOIDED.

The gr[e]ater future is the age of the space prophet
The scientific airy minded second man.
The prince of the power of the air.
The air is music.
The music is power.
The power of the past was its music.
The greater power of the future greater
     is its greater music.

Greater music is art.
Art is the foundation of any living culture.
Living culture is skilled culture
Skilled beautifulness, aim and care
And love of beauty is the only way to produce art.

Skilled culture is the new weapon of nations,
The new measure of determination as to whether a nation
Is ready to be a greater nation is art.
A nation without art is a nation without a lifeline.
Art is the lifeline because art is the airy concept
Of greater living. It is the airy foundation of the airy
Kingdom of the future.

TOMORROW BEYOND TOMORROW IS THE GREATER KINGDOM.

* This version was given to Salah Ragab in Egypt in 1984. The earlier version of this poem is "The Space Age Cannot Be Avoided".

The Potential (1965)

Beyond other thoughts and other worlds
are the things that seem not to be
And yet are.
How impossible is the impossible,
Yet the impossible is a thought
And every thought is real
An idea, a flash of potent fire
A seed that can bring to be
The reality of itself.
Beyond other thoughts and other worlds
Are the potentials . . .
That hidden circumstance
And pretentious chance
Cannot control.

The Potential (1972)

Beyond other thoughts and other worlds
Are the things that seem not to be
And yet are.
How impossible is the impossible
Yet the impossible is a thought
And every thought is real
An idea, a flash of intuition's fire
A seed of fire that can bring to be
The reality of itself.
Beyond other thoughts and other worlds
Are the potentials . . .
That hidden circumstance
And pretentious chance
Cannot control.

The Potential (1980)

Beyond other thoughts and other worlds
Are the things that seem not to be
And yet are.
How impossible is the impossible
Yet the impossible is a word; a thought
A thought . . . .
And every thought is real
An idea . . . . a flash of intuition's fire:
A seed of fire that can bring to be
The reality
Of its self.
Beyond other thoughts and other worlds
Are the potentials
That hidden circumstance
And pretentious chance
Cannot control.

Precision Fate

Too soon or too late
Is not the way-----
Precision fate
Is achievement done . . .
Precision fate
Is victory won;
Too soon or too late
Is not the way
When precision fate rules thus to say.

Different nations are really different notions
The alpha-omega equation is the code word-foundation
of this statement.
A notion is an idea
Every nation is really an idea
Every apparent thing is a living idea
Nature is an idea
The nature of a person is the vibration-idea or
Code of which a person is.
The nature of a thing
Is the property of a thing
Property is nature's place.

Preface

When I speak of wisdom
Differentiate . . . .
Behold!
One wisdom is the experience and the theory
Of the earth "life" you have known:
The earth tradition, the Life of man.
And the other wisdom
Is the wisdom from another plane
Of being . . . .
The other wisdom leads to Other Dimensions.

Prepare For The Journey (1980)*

This is the space-age . . . .
The age beyond the earth-age
A new direction
Beyond the gravitation of the past;.
This is the disguised twin of tomorrow
Striking upon the earth with relentless power
Like a perpetual whip.
This is the space age . . . .
Prepare for the journey;
You have a rendezvous
With the living wisdom
Of the unadulterated fate.
Prepare for the journey . . . .
  Like a happy child,
  You will step out of the pages
  Of the blinding blend of the book . . . .
  And gaze astounded at the endless space
  Of the cosmos-void.
  Your new course is the cosmic way
  Your new vehicle is the cosmic plane.
  You will learn to live the cosmo-way
  You will learn to journey with courage . . . .
  With fiery-aim
  To reach the splendour days
  Of the even greater tomorrow of the Cosmo-age.

* Two other versions of this poem are found under the title, "The Cosmic Age".

The Primary Enigma*

The primary enigma is the *being* and the *been* as
to differential relationship . . .
That which [has] been: [now] isn't
And that which be: [now] is

These are the words of the future
From the cosmic law
Of the united worlds.
That turn like jewels in the eternal sky
Thus it is spoken and thus it is.

[Editor note: *italicized* and [bracketed] words were added.]

* This poem without title appears at the end of a short essay by Sun Ra titled, "Comments and Poetry by Sun Ra" which was printed in an El Saturn Research pamphlet c.1978.

Primary Lesson: The Second Class Citizens (1968)

The second class is the second grade
And the second grade is the second dimension
of learning: Another phase of wisdom.

The second grade is the root of the
secondary education . . . . .
The secondary education is the
Higher form of wisdom,
The magnificent and advanced precept.
It is given as the Secondary Word
From the Secondary God
To the secondary citizens of the
Second Class.

To "on" the advance is to "own" the advance.
The Advance Prophet transcends the
Law concerning "A prophet."

Primary Lesson For Second Class Citizens (1972)

The second class is the second grade
And the second grade is the second dimension
Of learning another phase of wisdom.

The second grade is the root of the secondary education.
The secondary education is the higher form of wisdom,
The magnified and advanced precept.
It is given as the secondary word from the secondary to the secondary
This is the idea of the second woo.

To On the advance is to Own the advance.

There is no honor that earth can give to express in words or deeds
To compensate for heralded shame.
The earth itself is cursed, they say . . . .
The earth itself is cursed?
Its principle is dishonor then
Because its principle is dishonorable
And its principle is of the former things:
So that is why the glory it has given
Has been dishonor, because the glory of fame
Of the earth is dishonor even of the symbol of itself.
What price glory?
What glory is the price!
What a glory is the grace, what a grace, the glory is.

Prophecy

Advancements will be made
But it is to be of other dimensions
These advancements are beyond the measured.
They are advancement
It is outside as advancement always is.
The eternity/cycle/age code is circle
Return again according to the record
Repetition of the mirror existence
Yes, outside of the shadow world
Advancement shall be made
With giant strides
And lightning comprehension
Potential realization.

The Pure Sound

If you're not pure
Then you're not sound
Pure is real sincerity . . . .
And pure knows pure
Is sound and more than true.
Pure music is what you must face . . . . .
It's all what the music say of you;
It's not what the music you say of it.
If education systems fail,
It is not pure music's fault . . . . . .
In educations sanctuaries
Perhaps pure music still is not allowed.
If governmental systems fail . . . . . .
It is not pure music's fault
In government sanctuaries, too . . . . .
Pure music has no department berth.

Listen deeply to this and cogitate:
It is sound . . . . sound . . . sound
That makes the body sound . . . . .
    It is sound . . . . sound . . . . sound
    That makes the sound mind sound
 It is sound . . . . sound . . . sound . . . sound
 That makes the spirit besound . .
        A sound foundation is the key
        To locked-door fate's eternity . . .
        It is sound and sound again
        That makes the voice of silence heard.

The Quiet (1972)

Be quiet and speak not
Tho' yourself be wisdom incarnate
Be quiet
Tho' your mind be a roaring torrent of thought
Speak no more
Even when it is asked of you
Yes, be silent
Unless you speak in hidden meanings
And infinite timeless
Infinite phrases
Then those who are of intrinsic resemblance will understand
(and only those);
For the attunement of souls
and the attainment of friendly-brother friends
Is on the steppes of spirituel-worlds
A steppe, a step
A plain, dimension/plane.

The Quiet (1980)

Be quiet and speak not,
  'though yourself be wisdom incarnate . . . .
Be quiet . . . .
  'though your mind be a roaring torrent of thought.
Speak no more
  Even when it is asked of you.
Yes be silent -----------------
  Unless you speak in hidden meanings
    Infinite timeless phrases;
Then those of intrinsic resemblance will feel
  And understand . . . . Yes . . . Only those!
    For the attunement of souls
    And the attainment of
      Friendly-Brothership
        Is spirituel
        Eternally without compare . . . .

Rare Is

You drink in the beauty of all that is rare

All that can be never again

Not ever in the spiral-potentials of the Eternal Myth

Dwells there more than the only rare

Not even ever even of remembrance

Is there the duplicate of the only one

        rare is

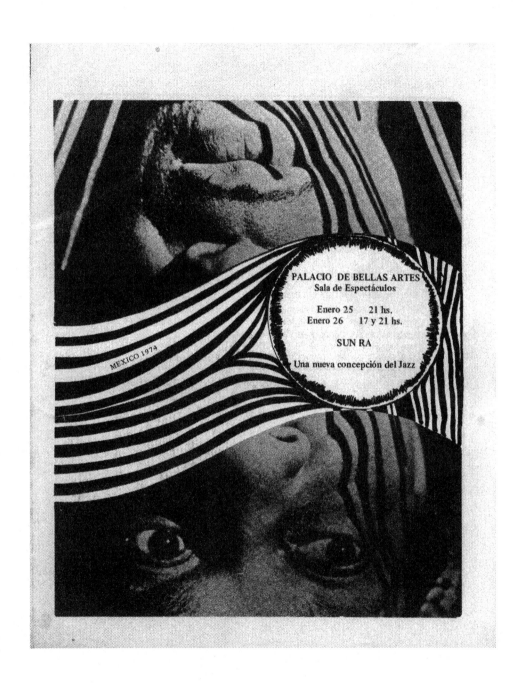

Re

Back in the backness of the blackness of the earth-black
        blackness backness
Back back in the backness re eternity-realm
        once-backness
I found blackness once was not the same as
        twice blackness duality
          I found
Thence decree was always was decree was I found
Their whole "life" through is nothing else but----------
Once - once - once - once was
An eternity eternal limitation outside of which
Everything else is nothing
Whence? why?
It is the decree from the world of once
It is not of the outer - greater worlds which are always is
But never once
For reflection is reflection
Thus there is the twiceness
Out to nothing
Out to O
Out tu O
Out two
Thus the twiceness reflection image im-niess-i-ness
A small one is equal to
Where is the where of when-ness then-ness
And why of the once is not the twice?
Ifness nonness isness
Ones is twice and it is
But one is once for ones is not the same as one's.
Over it is, ones is twice for it is two.

"Reality Has Touched Against Myth"*

Reality has touched against myth
Humanity can move to achieve the impossible
Because when you've achieved one impossible the others
Come together to be with their brother, the first impossible
Borrowed from the rim of the myth
Happy Space Age To You . . . .

* This poem appeared in the July 1969 *Esquire* with many other statements and poems by other celebrities for the occasion of the moon landing. The participants were asked to submit a statement that the astronauts should give when they set foot on the moon. Sun Ra is called here, "Sun-Ra (the space-age jazz poet)".

The Realm Of Myth (1972)*

A myth among other things
Is basically in the category of an idea
The vibration-radiation of an idea
Activates itself manisfested synchronization..

A lie among other things
Is basically in the category of a myth.

The myth is of images,
Because the myth and that which is of the myth
Is the activator of unlimited imagination
-----------Parallel to or more--------------
Synchronized to that which is not.

Everything is of a particular science
And myth is no exception.
Witness: 'Science-fiction'
And the manifestation of its self
To a living what is called reality
Or so-called reality.

As a science Myth has many dimensions
And many degrees.
Tomorrow is said to be a dimension of myth
Or even the very realm of myth itself

When it is said that
'Tomorrow never comes',
Thus when we speak of the future,
We speak of a lie,
Because the future is tomorrow
And tomorrow never comes.

* The 1980 version is identical except that the 1st and 4th stanzas are switched.

Resist Me! (1980)*

Resist me------------
Make me strong!
Resist me
Make me strong!
For since
I cannot be what you will . .
I will lean that much more
Toward what I will . . . .
Resist me--------------
Repulse my dreams!
Thus is a spark brought from nothing . . . .
Stone rubbed against stone
on the thirsty grass
  Dried and baked by a burning sun,
        Then suddenly: flame!
  Flame feeding flame!
      Now, nothing is the same . . .
      The stones are blackened;
          The grass is ashes . . . . . .
The pitiless sun is no less itself . . .
        But nothing is the same
                As before . . . .

* For an earlier version of this poem, see "Saga of Resistance".

Revolving Spheres (1972)*

Revolving spheres
Revolving spheres
Ornamented tinkling glass

Burnished gold and bronze
Remembrance . . . . .
Ah, to remember
Thought thought creatures
They are not of the earth-born
They are air-borne
Of sound and words
Flex their wings
Rush and run to and fro
Observing man
Observing man!

Thought thought creatures
Intellect unsurpassed by the earth-man
Laugh in their folded wings
Laugh in their leisure journey . . . . . constantly watching,
Constantly observing
Man.
Night and day.
They are of the between-world
Thought creatures of the between world
Not of this world
Not of any visible world
But another world-plane-dimension
Unbeknownst world

Fantastic, they say
Impossible,
And all the while, the anxious creatures
Watch . . .
Flex their wings
Pulling strings,
influencing the emotions,
The affairs of man.
These thoughts
      sometimes
           they flex their wings
                sail toward the dawn
                    sail toward the past
Move back and forth in time
Move back and forth
In dimensions
Superb Intellect
All the creatures
They always are
Long before man they are
Yet few men know of their existence
Few men pause to wonder
At their marvelous power
Their potent ever immortality
Their constant reiteration
that there are differentials of Evil
and some evils come from God.

* The 1980 version of this poem has the first two stanzas only.

The Rose Will Bloom

The rose will bloom
The broken bowl
Will never know
The perfect self
It once was shaped.
And though the heavens
Are as far from man
As all the past,
They are not lifeless
Or insensitive
As one would think . . . .
Seeing they are so distant;
Even as the past knows all the ways
Knows all the ways of man,
So the vast
And
Timeless firmament knows:
And being what it is,
It bides that we should search
For celestial-cosmo-truth of myth;
That we should know at last
Our true worth and insignificance
In proximity to the
Endless-Eternal Myth . . . .

Saga Of Resistance (1966)*

Resist me -------
Make me strong.
Resist me -------
Make me strong.
For since I cannot be what you will
I shall always be that much more so
What I will.
Resist me -------
Repulse my dreams
Thus is a spark brought from nothing . . . .
Stone rubbed against stone
Upon the thirsty grass,
Dried and baked by a burning sun** . . . .
Then suddenly: flame.
Flame feeding flame.
. . . Now, nothing is the same:
    The stones are blackened -------
     The grass is ashes
      The burning is still no less itself
       But all else is changed
       Nor ever shall be at it was before.

* For a later version, see "Resist Me", page 155.
** The version in Black Fire (1968) has this word as "son".

The Scale Of Nothingness

There came a whirl
And a throb in the spirit of the air
And the wind spoke to me . . . . .
"Every part of me is the essence of life . .
I came out from beyond
The comprehension of earth
There is no map of my realm.
My haven is the threshold and the Kingdoms
of the universe.
I live and dwell
As the scale of nothingness
For I am nothing
But I am power
And I am life itself."
Thus spoke the wind to me . . . .
While I listened to the music of the spheres.

The Self Of Negation

The self of complete negation
Is the point of no-ing oneself.
Death is semi-negation:
Life is semi-negation . . . . .
Together they make a positive aspect
When they are joined in at-onement . . . .
The onement of life and death is the end . . . .
And that is that particular weigh
Of the first shall be the last
Because the first is the one
And the beginning being the first is the end . .
Which is the last . . . .
That is the point: the aim or the end
Of the seekers of life:
Because life according to the accordingly
Is the betrothed of death;
And their rendezvous
Is continuous.
Beyond the veil of the rendezvous
The express-image of cosmo-ultra-light
Leaps to other places in the sky.

The Self Of Others

I do not question right
I do not question wrong
I only question questions . . . .
Because the answers
Speak for themselves . . . .
There is nothing hidden
To the unveiled eye;
If you can see yourself
You can see the self of others

Self Radiation

One day you will walk where I have walked;
Yet where I have walked,
I have walked seemingly in vain
And seemingly too all alone . . . .
Do not think I do not care . . . . .
I do . . . and that is the why of the Cosmo I,
The Omni-me myth mystery
Differentialed darkness dark sayings upon a harp . . . . .
The essence why of the why I am
A lonely weigh . . . a lonely path . . . a lonely way
Uncharted dimension-strange duality to that which is . . . . .
Yes, a lonely path I came to walk
More than the word itself could ever describe;
Yet . . . . . . do not despair
For myself is a many-multi-self
And along the way
I have left an alter-self-radiation
That will make its presence known
As you walk the way
To the place of the celestial weigh . . . .

The Shadow of the Fire (1966)

The vibrations of the sounds seem the same
But the meaning of the sounds
Take separate directions
At the crossroads
of the Cosmic-point of the arrow . . .
Beyond this Age
Through the darkness of the light years
And the light years of the darkness
Is the pure light of the pure darkness
And the pure darkness of the pure light.
The light is as the darkness
Because the light is the image
And the shadow of the fire.

The Shadow of the Fire (1972)

The vibrations of the sounds seem the same
But the meanings of the sounds
Take separate directions
At the crossroads
Of the cosmic-point of the arrow.

....

Beyond this age
Through the darkness of the light years
And the light years of the darkness
Is the pure light of the pure darkness
And the pure darkness of the pure light
The light is as the darkness
Because the light is the image
And the shadow of the fire.

The Shadow Of Tomorrow

Today is the shadow of tomorrow
Today is the present future of yesterday
Yesterday is the shadow of today.
The darkness of the past is yesterday,
And the light of the past is yesterday.
The days of yesterday are all numbered and summed in the
      word "once;"
Because "once upon a time there was a yesterday."
Yesterday belongs to the dead,
Because yesterday belongs to the past.
The past is yesterday.

Today is the prevue of tomorrow, but for me, only from a
      better and happier point of view.
My point of view is the thought of a better, untried reality.
Yesterday is eternity, the eternity of yesterday is dead.
Yesterday is as one, the eternity of one is the eternity of the past.
The past is once upon a time, once upon a time is past, the past
      is yesterday.

The light of the past is the light which was,
The wisdom of the past is the light of the past;
The light of the future is the light which is to be,
The wisdom of the future is the light of the future.

Yesterday belongs to the dead, tomorrow belongs to the living.
The past is certified as the finished product, anything which is
    ended is finished.
That which is perfect is finished, the perfect man is no exception
    to the rule.
The perfect man of the past is made according to the rule of the
    past.
The rule of the past is the law of injustice and hypocrisy.
The revelation of the meaning of the law is revealed through the
    law itself.

The wisdom of the past is the light of the past
The light which is to be is the wisdom of the future
The light of the future casts the shadow of tomorrow.

The Skilled Way

Being is the attribute or derivative of
The root-word "be".

. . . . Art is the skilled way . . . the skilled weigh
Because it is the weigh of skill . . . .

Art is the principle of the potential of
The mind and the principle of the natural-real
Being on the advanced plane/view of
The alter reality.
The alter-reality is of the angelic-revelation.
This reason (angelic) sometimes takes
The form of wheels of light and when these
Wheels of light begin to turn,
Particular dimensions of power are generated
Into the mind-spirit of those
Whose mind-spirits are tuned to the sound of
The voice of the wheels.

Then again, the alter-reality magnifies itself
To be the light of the Cosmos.
The Cosmos is the ever Eternal or the never
Ending immeasureable. That immeasureable
Beingness of the Cosmos is abstract art
Beyond compare.
. . . . The vibrating synonym of/for IS, AM, ARE, BE
And Eternal is ON. The poetical word for are is
Art. Art is IS. To this very day the LORD'S
Prayer reads: "Our father which art in heaven"

Some Tomorrow (1972)*

Some tomorrow-the potential word
Not the same tomorrow's tomorrow of today
But a greater far-reaching
Living design
Beyond the limit of that which only always was.
Some tomorrow
That we know we own
That is on the way
To other mountains,
Even mountains beyond
The mountains of this one earth.
Mountains of other dimensions
Other planes and planets.

Some tomorrow
Not the same tomorrow
Not the same tomorrow
That is still the past
Disguised under other names;
No, not that tomorrow
But some other better tomorrow,
That never came before . . .
Some rare-myth-fiction of outer-thought
Adventure is

* Another version from 1973 is called "From Tomorrow".

Some Tomorrow (1980)*

Some tomorrow
Not the same yesterday's tomorrow
That now they call today.
Some other tomorrow's tomorrow
Living Cosmo design of Omni-Everness
Beyond the limit of that which only always was;
Some tomorrow that we know we own.
Some tomorrow that is on its way to other mountains;
Even mountains beyond
The mountains of this one earth . . . . . .
Mountains of other planes
Other dimensions and planets.
Some tomorrow, not the same yesterday's tomorrow
No! . . . . . Not the same tomorrow of the past:
The recurring oath-sword-cycle curse
Not that same false-tomorrow
That is still the past disguised under other names.
No!
Not that tomorrow, but some better tomorrow
That never came before
A mystic-magic gift of all gifts
A rare myth-fiction-outer-thought
Intuition-feel adventure.

* Another version from 1973 is called "From Tomorrow".

Somewhere Else

Once I thought the world was somewhere else
Twice I looked and saw the world was still there
In its improper place
Boldly standing there for all the world to see
It is not somewhere else
But still in its improper place.

The Sound I Hear (1972)

The sounds I hear are nothing
They seem to be but are not,
These walls around me are nothing
They seem to be but are nothing,
This ceiling above me
Is nothing
If I would, I could learn the how
An[d] see through it
And challenge the sky
And all its myriad worlds
These seeming emotions, so real, so enlightning
That gently speak to me
Are nothing
They seem to be but are nothing
These sometime bewilderments,
These haunting memories
Yesterdays
And yesterday's now
How unlike the days I would to be
How unlike the days I would to horizon-be the future.
But this is the alter-future I speak of.
The alternative is the key.

The Sounds I Hear (1980)

The sounds I hear are nothing,
    They seem to be but are not.
These walls around me are nothing,
    They seem to be but are nothing . . . .
This ceiling above me is nothing;
      If I would,
        I could learn the how and see through it . . . . . .
          Challenge the sky and all its mansions
          Of myriad worlds.

These seeming emotions . . . . so real . . .
     . . . . . . Deep intrigues of charm . . . .
That gently speak to me are nothing:
        They seem to be but are nothing . . . .
These sometimes bewilderments,
These haunting memories of yesterdays then
        And yesterdays now . . .
This now is only the reality of yesteryears shadow . . . . . .
        That came before . . . .
How unlike the days I would to be . . . .
How unlike the tomorrows that never came this way . . . .
      Tomorrow never touches the shores of a world
         Of yesterdays
      Tomorrow never touches the shores of a world
         Of Yesterday.

SUN-RA

INTERGALAXTIC RESEARCH
P. O. BOX 7124
CHICAGO, ILLINOIS, 60607

The Sound Image . . (1972)*

That's what the music says, that is how I say the music . . . .
The music is a journey, the journey is endless
It is sound endlessness communication language point.
Endless sound is a universal language because that is what the music is
Equations bridge across the bridgeless-bottomless world of sound
That is what the music is, the universal language
The bridge-communication sound.
There is no other way to speak to everyone in language each can
Feel and understand except through music.
    How can you speak to other worlds except through the music, the
music lets them know, where you are at and what you are.
If you are pure, the music's pure.
The music is your testing ground, it is your choice that tells the tale,
When all else fails.

    Pure music is what you must face.
    If you limit, if you reject, if you do not consider
    If you are selfish-earthly bound,
    Pure music is your nemesis.
        You cannot pretend: you will accept or you will reject.
        There is no middle ground.
The mirror of pure music is a negative field/feel that photographs
   The image-mind-impression soul and psychic-self even the potential
     immediate alter-destiny/destinies.

The music is the image is the music is the image
The sound image.
The living image of sound . . . . Image
Sound of the Cosmo-World approach journey.
The waves of sound are like waves of water in the ocean
There is a tide and time of sound
This the music is like a journey
Which is endless
Unscheduled directions are suddenly necessary
Now and then to syncronize the code momentum dimension

To environmental light or darkness equation-balance image
Or** improvisational alter counterpoint blueprint sound.
The music is not only just music.
It touches and projects other dimensions
Time-zone eternities and cosmo-infinity spiral-parallels
The parallels are feels/fields of parables, which are instruments
For the instruments are not only just instruments
The people are the instrument.
That's how the music goes, that's what the music is . . . .

That is the mirror on the wall, above the handwriting there. It is invisible
                to all
It is a mirror that you must hear
Vibration . . . rhythm . . . . harmonic sound is hidden in each melody.
It is never what it seems to be
You can only hear what the mirror sees. No more, nor less is ever allowed.
The sound mirror is what you see of you that's sound.
      If you're not sound,
      Then you're not pure
Pure is real-sincerity
    and pure knows pure is sound and true.
                It's all what the music says of you
                It's not what the music you say of it.
IT'S ALL WHAT THE MUSIC SAYS OF YOU
    The music is the living mirror of the universe.

* The 1980 version is nearly identical except for punctuation and spacing.
** This word is not in the 1980 version.

The Sound Meaning

The product and the producer concerns me
As to whether either are independent agents
In this instance, I mean music and musicians.
Whence cometh they?
From somewhere brilliantly sound
For since I hear the music
Upon the beam I trace the sound
And always the beam vibrates
The meaning of the sound.

Sound Myth

After the myth comes the origin or
After the origin is the end
Comes the myth.
This myth is descriptive.
It is either one or the other except for
The in-between, which is a seeming
Neutral point.

Sound/Silence (1972 - IE Vol.I)

What can I say other than the music itself?
Music?
Yes, to the ears that dare to hear
That dare to hear
Both the silence and the sound!
Music?
Yes, the silence/sound duality necessity belongness . . . Balanced
projection pointless
Cosmo-Nature/natural feeling sensitivity
Dial pointer vibration-intensity indicator
Express image expression need necessity being code alter-
otherness continuance
Continuance On . . On . .On
The music is in the word of words ON . . . .

[Sound/Silence]

(1972- Space Is The Place LP Jacket)

What can I say other than the music itself?
Music?
Yes, to the ears that dare to hear, that dare to hear, that dare to hear,
Both the silence and the sound.
Music?
Yes, the silence sound
Duality necessity belongness
Balanced projection pointless cosmo nature natural feeling-
sensitivity
Dial point of vibration intensity
Indicator express image expression
Express image expression need necessity being
Code alter-otherness continuance . . . on
On . . on . .on
The music is the word of words . . . on

The Sounds Of Planets

In the same way that a certain sound in one
Particular language is equal to a different
Meaning in another language, so the sounds on
One planet which equal a particular thing
On that one planet is equal to another thing
On another planet. It might mean the exact
Opposite or it might mean something entirely
Unrelated according to the orthodox standards
Of the related.

The Space Age Cannot Be Avoided (1957)*

The prophets of the past belong to the past
The space prophets of the greater future
Belong to the greater future.
The greater future is the age of the Space Prophet,
The scientific airy-minded second man:
The prince of the power of the air.
The air is music.
The music is power.
The power of the past was its music,
The greater power of the future greater
Greater music is art,
Is its greater music:
Art is the foundation of any living culture.
Living culture is skilled culture
Skilled dutifulness, aim and care
And love of beauty is the only way to produce art.
Skilled culture is the new weapon of nations,
The new measure of determination as to whether a nation
Is ready to be a greater nation is art.
A nation without art is a nation without a lifeline.
Art is the lifeline because art is the airy concept
Of greater living. It is the airy foundation of the airy
Kingdom of the future.
Tomorrow Beyond Tomorrow is the greater kingdom,
THE KINGDOM OF THE SPACE AGE . . .

* A later version of this is found as "Points on the Space Age" (1984), page 139.

The Spiral Way

Man is the same as he ever was
He ever could do . . .
He ever could be
He ever could come to be
According to his desire for liberty . .
He has not perused the words,
"Make him free"
Request of one in enmity.
Man has not chanced to realize
The snares of liberty are supervised.
To know is differential reach sublime
Intuition's balanced weigh . . . . . .
Being of a higher spirit than he knows,
Wh[e]n he comes to know . . . he shall be
What at last he knows himself to be:
From nothing to nothing to nothing
To nothing beyond
  He activates the spiral way.

Spirituel (1971)

They have a labyrinth in their head
To open is magic
To close without is a spiral otherness
And sin is always at the door
Wherever there is someplace else
And some place however not
Point is . . . . the exquisite dimension
And nothingness prevails always before
And after ever is beyond
The limited end
For such eternity
Mathematic symbolization
Countdown zero
Is but a stepping stone
As every eternity is
To other ways and means
Prince and principality
Diamond rule and arch-authority

Spirituel (1980)

They have a labyrinth in their head
To open is magic;
To close without is of spiral otherness
And sin is always at the door . . . .
Wherever there is some place else
And some place however not,
Point is . . . .
The exquisite dimension and nothingness
Prevails always before and after ever is beyond
The limited not;
For such eternity . . . . mathematic-symbolization
Countdown zero is but a stepping stone . . . .
As every eternity is
To other ways and means . . . .
Prince and principality
Diamond rule and arch-authority.

The Spontaneous Love (1972)

The spontaneous love is the idea that is to be,
Like the light of a fire it beams bright
And its warmth casts rays into every shadow of the mind.
It lives and blossoms like the flaming petals of a cosmic-flower.
It never dies because it is the idea of that which is to be
And that which is to be cannot die
Because only that which "was" was fated to die.
That which is is the idea of the future
Is the light of the future;
But that which was is the shadow of the past.
There is nothing new under the sun of the past,
That is why the history therein repeats itself.
The circle is the cycle and
The cycle is the eternity thereof.

The name of the unending circle
Is the circle that is not a circle
Yet is a continual circle,
The symbol of that which is eternal
Is an onward sense
Rather than that which was
Which is an idea of eternity
In an inward never-is-sense.

The Spontaneous Love (1980)

The spontaneous love is the idea of that which is to be.
　　Like the light of a fire it beams bright
　　　　And its warmth casts rays
　　　　　　Into every shadow of the mind . . . .
　　　　　　It lives and blossoms
　　　　　　　　Like the flaming petals of a cosmic flower.
　　　　　　　　It never dies
　　　　　　　　Because it is the idea of that which is to be
　　　　　　　　And that which is to be yet is not
　　　　　　　　Cannot die . . . .
Only that which "was"
　　　　Was fated to die.
　　　　Earth's history is the wasness of things
　　　　　　That is why the history repeats itself.
　　　　　　History is the cycle of an eternity.

The cycle is a circle of limitation
　　When the circle is of itself . . . . . one.
　　　　There is an unending circle
　　　　　Which is symbolic of continuation Eternal continuum.
　　　　　Expressed by the ever-outward
　　　　　　Reaching spiral
　　　　　　　Of the Omni-Cosmos.

The Spontaneous Mind

Walk toward the brilliant circles of tomorrow
　　That turn each other . . . .
　　Wheel turning wheel;
For every wheel is the will
　　And the will is the power
　　　　Of the fire
　　　　Of the spontaneous mind . . . . .

The Stage Of Man

Once there was a man who lived for God;
Now where is a man who lives for man?
That he who lives for man may speak
To he who lived for God
And thereby man (each man among men) will live
In freedom from the tyranny of man
From the stupidity among men
From the brutality of darkness
And let sound-reasoning in a cosmic sense
Be the light treasured above all else
On earth
That man might rise above the stage of man

The Sub-Dwellers (1972)

Down in the subterranean places of the city
Down in the catacombs and caverns of the mind
Down,
Down in the earth catastrophe of knowledge
Dwell they, the sub-dwellers . . .
Of alter-mind we syncronize
To them, the sub-dwellers, BY QUICKENING TO US . . . . .
Their potential need . . . their great emergency
Within seeds they seem
Like enseeded rocks and roots hidden from the sun
Down, down must go to them the dawn
The loving heat of the sun
To touch them with immortal rays
The on-ness reach demands it be
. . . rays to envelope them like a net of kindly prisms . . .
They will be, they will come forward to the two-wardness of the
Intuition of the On
For it is On that is.
The voice of the greater universe will draw them
To Chromatic vibrations of the Is isness
They will come forward from whence, whereever they are
They shall come forward to the sound of sounds
Yes, A sound of sound will burst the oath of earth asunder
A projective aim to blast the secret The cruel citadel . . .
Yea, even the coded seed will open its walls
And that unmeant secret place will be no more their home
For out of the earth-darkness
They shall come forward dancing to the sound beams of dark rays of light
And they will rise to the heavens of the natural skies
There they will be like the fires of the rays
And the rays of the sound of the sun.

The Sub-Dwellers (1980)

Down in the subterranean places of the city
Down in the catacombs and caverns of the mind
Down . . . down in the earth catastrophe of knowledge
Dwell they the sub-dwellers . . . .
Of alter-mind we syncronize atune their spirit self
By quickening them to us and alter-destiny . . . .
We see their potential need . . . their great emergency
Within seeds they seem like enseeded rocks and roots
Hidden from the sun.
Down . . down . . down must go them the dawn
Of the loving heat of the sun
To touch them with immortal rays
The On-ness reach demands it be
Rays to envelope them like a net of kindly prisms . . . . . .
They will be . .
They will come forward to the two-wardness
Of the intuition of the On . . . . .
For it is On that Is.
The voice of the greater universe will draw them
To Chromatic Vibrations of the Is Isness . . .
They will come forward from whence,
Wherever they are . . . . . .
They will come forward to the sound of sounds
Yes,
A sound of sound will burst the oath of earth asunder:
A projective aim to blast the secret place of woe . . . .
The cruel citadel . . . .
Yea, even the coded seed will open it's walls
And that unmeant secret place will be no more their home;
For out of the earth darkness
They shall come forward dancing to the sound beams
Of dark rays of light
And they will rise to the heavens of the natural skies
There they will be like the fires of the rays
And the rays of the sound of the sun.

The Substitute Words

How carefully laid the scenes
How brilliantly superimposed
The substitute words to say and do.
How forced the seeming way of the pseudo-life.
If they would believe that vanity has them captive
If they would but believe the earth-gravity
Has them chained to its earth-plane vibration
Then they would come to know
Beyond the thing they call
The Beginning and End of knowledge-wisdom
They would come to know
And they would know they know.

Sun-day

This is my day
A sunny day
This is my day
A sunny day
With so much to give to all
Bright beams
Striking at the shadows impartially.
This is my day
I have so much to say

Out of the sun colors come
Like spores the rays strike the earth
And forms of being take shape to be
Being raises itself accordingly
To the vibration of the ray to which it synchronizes itself.

The invisible light is the ultra-light . . . . the darkness
The darkness is the cosmo-light . .
The all pervading all
Thus the cosmo-equation of the light
Is that the darkness is as the light
So distinguish the meaning of this
And ultra BE: an Ultra-Being.

Synchronization Inverse

A secret hidden power of kindness

And gentle love seeming to be

War and viciousness is

A misinterpreted form

Of tender mercies

According to the earth plane of the earth wicked

Who have neither seen the outward plane

Nor heard the sound of the voice

They do not understand

But activate according

The synchronization inverse or myth

Tale

As the tale is told
It is tolled
And this is the weigh
For it is the total or the sum
The sum is the all: Pan.

Pan: All
That is as is
The nation of All
The nation of Pan
Nature's God.

THE -------O------L O G Y . . . .

The o logy concerns the o.
The o is the earth
The oath is the curse, the oath, the word
The earth is the erth, the eorthe,
the orth/oith/oth . . . the o . . the o/oeth/oat
The earth is three/thre
And X is three from the end of the alphabet . . . zyx . . . Z-Y-X . . . . . .
Now X is C because C is the initial
But X is sometimes used instead
C is three and X is three.

The O . . the cipher . . the code
The code X . . the codex . . the law
The cipher is lu cipher
The Le is Lu because The is Thu
The cipher: Lucipher: Lucifer . . . .

The Three Dimensions Of Air

Air is Space
Air is Melody
Air is Manner or Spirit
It is the air that we breathe
That is important to the active existence
Of ourselves
Likewise it is the air
That we listen to
That is important to the active existence
Of our minds
And it is the air
That is the important point
    Of the state of the cultural life of an
    individual or nation.
The spirit of things is the way of things
And the way of things is the manner of
    things
Is the active state of things
And the state is the word
Because 'to word' something is to state it.
    To word To state
    Word State
    Word Ward
    To word Toward
    To word Toward   on

To Outer Unseen Worlds

Come my brother, you are dear to me
I will take you to new worlds
Greater in splendor than anything earth possesses.
If you are fearful, you are of the futile persuasion
If you are strong, you will be as I
I am nothing
My symbol is the name of nothing
And yet I speak as the living pattern
for the spirit.
The spirit is as I
Nothing can withstand my will
I cover the earth
And hold it like a ball in my hand
I can dash it to bits if I will
Or with the power of my forces
I can take it in seconds
To another galaxy
And set it gently in another place.

To the Peoples of Earth

Proper evaluation of words and letters
In their phonetic and associated sense
Can bring the peoples of earth
Into the clear light of pure Cosmic Wisdom.

Tomorrow's Vibrations

One by one, my children left me;
    My shadow children. My images of the light.
I had tried to school them with a parable;
Then I tried to school them
        With the incomparable . . . . .
    But they left me.
Now I dwell alone;
And in my shadow loneliness,
        I reach into the dark
    And in quiet unseenness
Separate the darkness from the dark . . . .
For the darkness
        Is only a segment of the dark: :
A cycle willed to simulated-life . . . . .
    Enscrolled; . . As pre-determined fate,
        And each cycle of darkness . . . .
            I change through magic
            The living magic of my word!
    The multi-principle . . . potential-impossibility
    Changing the darkness into beingness . . . .
    I shall press the darkness-dark into form . . .
    And the form shall be nothingness:
        A space-spore of mystic potential . . . . .
Then suddenly I shall touch the darkness
        With sound thought
        Of tomorrow's vibrations.
    Vibrations which are ultra-eternal.
    Thus causing those whom I choose to be
    Ultra-Eternal-Living-Sound Omni-Beings.

The Tone of Abstract Love

Prelude . . . . Prelude
The shadowy light bursts into flame-fire
Myth-fire living . . . . . living . . . . living . . . . .
Burning plane sun-dimensions

Prelude . . . . . Prelude . . . . Outer
Darkness is the darkness dark
Itself to be the synonym
Of brilliant chromatic lights and fire,
Thus the shadow come to be
They take shape, they are to be
Shadows take shape and dance
Dance to the tune of Abstract Love.

The Tradition Creator

The delusion is the God - idea . . . . . .
The deception is the conception-certified
        Or the certified conception of the God-idea
Cast the outworn God-idea out of your mind
    The outworn God-idea
        Is the control center
        Which has been used to mold the minds
            Of the complacent, the unwary
                And the unsuspecting . .
        It has destroyed the innocent
                As well as
            Trapped the guilty . . . .
            The outworn God-idea
            Has really been the creator
    Of the world as it is today . . . .

The Tree is Wood

The tree is wood
Would you to know? Would you to know,
The things you would to think you should?
You Would?
I thought you would.
I thought you would . . . I thought you would.
The tree is wood, it's would you know
But that's a saying deep and dark
I mean the wood is tree is wood
    Would the meaning of you would?
The will, the would upon the wood
The wood . . . look at the dictionary's Wood.
I think you should, I think you should
To know the meaning, I think you should
To know the meaning of the wood
Don't forget the wood is wood
Look up the word, the pecker word
Behold the pecker . . . spirit . . . would
The pecker would. The pecker would

Behold the pecker, peckerwood.
Peckerwould, peckerwood
Spirit wood, spiritwood
Peter wood, peckerwood
Pecker: pick, a pecker/pick . . . picker, pecker . . peckers peck
Peckers pick/discriminate
They choose to choose
I wish you would
I wish you would to choose to choose
A pecker would
I think you should.
Watch out! There're different kinds of wood
Somebody's would is out to lunch
They're out to lunch, but that's their wood. The would . . . . .
The wood . . . the tree is wood
Don't let them get you on a tree
A wooden beam, a bush (ambush) . . Behold, beware, take extra care
Don't wander out upon a limb, a limb, a lamb, a lamb a limb
Be careful of the branch, the branch . . . A pecker would, a wormwood too.
Peckerwood: wormwood too. Thus is my would I think you should.

Truth Is Bad Good (1972)

Truth is bad
Or truth is good
It depends upon where
And why and how and who you are.

The word truth must be considered carefully
And the precepts of that which is called truth
Must be equationized and balanced
And understood.
Or else, it must be abandoned
And another truth placed in its place.
This is the idea of the greater age
The outer worlds of etherness*
This is the word from the Cosmic-Cosmo-Tomorrow.

* This entire line was ommitted in the 1980 version, "Truth: Bad: Good"

The Truths That Should Not Be

The truths used as the foundation
Of the world today
Is not the truth that should be the truth,
It is not the natural truth
It is an adapted-adopted truth

That is why I speak of myth . . . .
There are different kinds of myth
But sometimes they touch each other
Like realities
When they are in proximity to each other; ;
At times they can see each other
Or feel each other's presence/presences
When they pass each other by
In different directions
Or are parallel to each other
In moving eternities
Symbols,
Projections or related consequences.
The simplicity of everything is involved
Because of its derivative multiplicities . . . . .
So only if you know
Can you compare equationally
For advanced onwardness . . . .
The experience indicates
That to rise from the valueless
To the omni-valueless is the epi-cosmic idea
Invaluable . . . .

Twice Told (1972)

I told you once,
You did not see . . .
I mentioned
Immortality

I TOLD YOU ONCE, YOU DID NOT SEE, I MENTIONED
        I M M O R T A L I T Y . . . .

I   TOLD   YOU   ONCE
   YOU   DID   NOT   SEE
        THE   WORD
             IS
I M   M   O   R   T   A   L   I   T   Y   !

Twice Told (1980)

I told you once,
You did not see . . . .
I mentioned: immortality
I TOLD YOU ONCE, YOU DID NOT SEE
I M E N T I O N E D I M M O R T A L I T Y . . . .
I   TOLD   YOU   ONCE
       THEN ONCE AGAIN
            THE   WORD
                 IS
I M   M   O   R   T   A   L   I   T   Y

Twin Vibrations (1972)

The vibrations are
These images are twins
They draw, they sketch,
They figure, they blueprint

The myriad destiny fates.

Vibrations sound both heard and unheard
Vibrations both seen and unseen
Infinite presence
Deep highway rays of communication
With/to the All universe
Even its unknown duality phases.

If it is to see, to be, to know:
The vibration will let you know
The vibration will let you see.
The vibration will let you be
The vibration will let you be.

Twin Vibrations (1980)

These images are twins
They draw, they sketch,
They figure, they blueprint
Vibrations Sound both heard and unheard
Vibrations both seen and unseen
Infinite presence
Deep highway rays of communication
With/to the All universe
Even its unknown duality phases.

If it is to see, to be, to know:
The Vibration will let you know
The Vibration will let you see.
The Vibration will let you be
The Vibration will let you be.

The Ultimate All

Sometimes
  All is not all;
    Because
      The COSMOS-ALL is the ALL-ALL . . . .
    It is the
      "THE ULTIMATE" ALL
         Of
    The Omni-universes
There are different kinds of all
I speak of a different kind of ALL . . . .

The Universe Sent Me
To Converse With You (1972)

The universe sent me to converse with you
If there are ears to hear, listen, but do not listen with yours ears
alone
You must feel with your intuition-sense.
It is always the unknowing-knowing voice of the quiet-vigilant
silence.
Your intuitional-intuition sense.
The universe sent me to converse with you.

This planet is a perfect place, according to its own decision code
But still there is something missing here, a greater need than all
the rest.
A need long hidden from earth-guards gaze,
A need of giant-imperative now
It cannot be: it will not be denied.

This need's coordinate-would-wish-desire
I speak to you for nature sent me too
Another gift to offer you
And music: Nature's - Natural-Master's -creation voice
Is one of the bridges to the treasure-house

Of needs fulfilled.
What and how are you?
I send my warmest greetings
From the where of the Cosmo-usual
I am doing what I am supposed to do,
I am being what I am supposed to be.
It is a strange circumstance, like being upon an alien-planet-world
All alone . . . . . But I am not alone, there are ears to hear even here
There are ears that will listen with mind-soul's-spirit pure
Of those,
For those who are in tune with Nature's Cosmo-plan-plane-design
Can hear what untuned ears cannot
And those who hear will know the meaning of the natural-beist.
The Living Being-Beist
The Space sea has many sounds of be-isness:
The akasa, the unknown acoustics, the alter planes of isness and notness
Are all a part of everything,
The everything and the nothingness.
See the sound-riddle of the double-beast.

The Universe Sent Me (1980)

The universe sent me to converse with you . . . .
If there are ears to hear . . . listen;
But do not listen with your ears alone . . . .
You must feel with your intuition-sense;
   It is always the unknown-knowing voice
    Of the quiet-vigilant silence
  Your celestial connection sense . . . .
The universe sent me to speak and say:
This planet earth is a perfect place
For those who according to-ed
 An executed decision-code . . . .
But still there is something missing here . . . .
A need long hidden from earth-guards gaze;
 Of greater need than all the rest
   Cannot will not longer be denied.
It is of this need's coordinate-wish-desire
I speak to you . . . . . . for nature sent me too,
Another gift to offer you:
The omni-touch of music-lore
The natural Master's Creator voice
The bridge of sound-vibration path
To the treasure-house of needs fulfilled.
What dimension thence are you?
Whither whence thou goeth?
I will not ask again . . if answers you have none.
Still, I send my warmest greetings
From the where of the Cosmos-rare:
I am being what I am supposed to be . . . .
Like an alien-being alone upon an outcast world.
But I am not alone; there are ears to hear even me.

The Unknown State (1972)

In a world which does not know God
It is sometimes better for a God
To pretend there is no God
Then because no God is non-existent
The no-God is by the non-existent laws
The unwritten laws of the non-existent
        state
The unknown state
Beyond the guarded boundaries of
      a place prepared:
The house of the version.
In some strange realm
That never was
But always is
The no-God
Came to know-God.
Thus they met in abstract-friendship,
Beyond the road of the mills of the
        gods,
By the Bypass
Of the valley of the shadow;
Because the extinction
Of the non-existent
Is impossible
And that which is impossible
Is always
The idea that lingers on.

The Unknown State (1980)

In a world which does not know God
It is sometimes better for a God
To pretend there is no God

Then, because the no-God
Is of the Kingdom of that which is not . . . .
The no-God is the superior non-existent
In the kingdom which is not: . .Yet is.
The unwritten laws of the unknown state
Is authorized law in a not-way.
Beyond the guarded boundaries
Of a place prepared:
The house of the virgin-version

In some strange realm
That never was
But always is
The no-God
Came to know-God.
Thus they met in abstract-friendship,
Beyond the road of the mills of the
                                    gods,
By the Bypass
Of the valley of the shadow;
Because the extinction
Of the non-existent
Is impossible

The impossible is always the idea
        That lingers on.

Unremembered Dreams (1957)

Unremembered dreams
Linger, . . . pensive . . . poignant.
Unremembered dreams
Cleverly evasive
Haunt the path of hidden thought,
Walk the streets of beauty
And pull at tangled threads
That seek to weave themselves
Into the fabric and flare of life.

Unremembered Dreams (1980)

Unremembered dreams
Linger - pensive - poignant
Unremembered dreams
Stolidly evasive
Haunt the pathway of tangled threads
That weave themselves into the fabric of life.

Unseen Definition (1972)

It is not right for those to speak to me
To speak of freedom
Who have the wrong definition of freedom
It is not right for those to speak to me
To speak of love
If they have never felt the meaning of love

Love and freedom
What words they are
Yet look at the fruits of the action thereof
Is this life all that life should be?
Consider . . . . .
Freedom itself can be an empty shell
Without a greater cause
For just as an empty shell is free
Without inner substance
So can one be
If freedom is another word
For an unseen definition
Of a principle in secret code.

Unseen Definitions (1980)

It is not right
    For those to speak to me
      To speak of love
        If they have never felt
        The meaning of love . . . .
It is not right
    For those to speak to me to speak of freedom
      Who have the wrong definition of freedom . . . .
    What good is freedom's liberty
      If sword and famine
        Pestilence is its creed . . . . . .
        Proclamated by God
          An unfailing promised heritage . . .

    Love and freedom
  What words are they!
  The events of the world today are the fruits thereof . . .
Yes . . Look at the fruits of the actions thereof.
Is this life all that life should be?
      Consider . . . . .
Freedom itself can be an empty shell
    Without a greater cause . . . .
      For just as an empty shell is free
    Without inner substance
    Likewise can a person be
If freedom is really in this era of time
    A hidden code of an unseen definition.
    A trigger word of tragic illusion.

Victory Dual

Some things are true
And
Some things are not . . . . .
While others are neither:
They are dimensions of potentials
The potential subdivide
Into immeasurable contractions
And Immeasurable expansion expression.
The odds against
Can be balanced into dual victory
For victory is balanced
When it wins on both sides . . . .
The four negatives symbolizes
40 days 40 nights which are 40.
The forty consecutively centered
Are 4 ways and 4 powers.
The four ways are directional
Intent, the 4 powers are
Diminished mights represented by the little ones.
The forty little
Ones are represented by the lV. The l
With the V for victory not the
Dramatized earth victory: but the cosmos mystery
Victory
Which is eternal
Beyond man's unauthorized control.

Visions Out

Metamorphosis Vision
Transmolecular light
Transcendent darkness rule/measure of the outerness
Black, chromatic
Synthesis on
It is yon diamond project differential
Sapphire beam ruby
Gem-Gemini
Plane transcendent/visions out.

The Visitation

In the early days of my visitation,
Black hands tended me and cared for me . . .
Black minds, hearts and souls loved me . . .
And I love them because of this.
In the early days of my visitation,
Black hands tended me and cared for me;
I can't forget these things.
For black hearts, minds and souls love me--
And even today the overtones from the fire
of that love are still burning.
In the early days of my visitation
White rules and laws segregated me . . .
They helped to make me what I am today
And what I am, I am.
Yes, what I am, I am because of this
And because of this
My image of paradise is chromatic-black.
And chromatic-black again.
Those who segregate did not segregate in vain
For I am,
And I am what I am.

Voice of the Timeless Spirit . . .

What can I do to help the world?
What could I do?
It is not my world.
Or at least I think it isn't.
Have I forgotten something?
Am I to blame?
Did I create this?
What did I do wrong?
Why does the creation groan and suffer?
If I can help in any way
Should I?
We do not accept each other.
I have so much to offer them.
What do they have to offer me?
They are spiritually poor. I have sympathy
For them, they have no sympathy for me.
What can I do?
I do not wish that they should think or say
I am their god but if I help them - what would
They say?
They have been
Alone so long.

We Hold This Myth To Be Potential (1972)

We hold this myth to be potential
    Not self evident alone but equational;
      Another Dimension
         Of another kind of Living Life
            Abstract-Projection Presence
This Myth are these
We be potential
    This myth is not what you know
What you know is the knowledge
Beyond that is the separate of the ignorance
The greater wisdom is the unknown ignorance
You do not know and that is the knowledge beyond the knowledge
For beyond the knowledge is the Infinity:
The uncharted ignorance.
You cannot measure that which is the ignorance;
Because of your limitation, you are of the limited ignorance
If you are only of the earth mind
You have not as yet seen
You have not seen
That there is a mirror
Between you and the universe;
And all you see is your reflection
Because of that reflection-thought.

We Hold This Myth To Be Potential (1980)

We hold this myth to be potential
    Not self evident but equational:
  Bridge-doorway
      Abstract projection-presence
        Omni-dimension direction
          To another kind unknown Living Live-Life.
        This myth are these
    This myth are and is
    We be potential
    This myth is not that which you know . . . .
      What you know is the knowledge
        But beyond that is the separate of the ignorance.
        The greater wisdom is the unknown-ignorance
        Which you do not know . . . .
        And is the knowledge beyond the knowledge
        For beyond the knowledge is the infinity:
        The uncharted ignorance.

    You cannot measure that which is the ignorance;
    Thus because of your limitation,
   You are of the limited ignorance . . . .
If you are only of the earth mind
You have not as yet seen
  That there is a mirror between you and the universe;
    And all you see is your reflection-thought.

What You So! (1972)

This today is judgement day
A ruler rules the judgement be
This day to judge
Today is judgement day
Too long delayed but yet
Are you too blind to the evils of non-discrimination
That you dare not understand?
Are you so willfully ignorant of what you should be;
That you think you are only what others say
                    you are,
Yet perhaps you fail to realize
That what you are
you are
And thus so approve or so, Thusly,
If what you reap is what you so
What you reap is what you are:
Amen!
Because what you 'am' is what to be
And what you is, you am
And what you be, you are
If what you are is what you so.
Am - in
Amen!
Am -on
Amen!

What You So! (1989)*

This today is a judgement day
It is more likely, examination day.
A ruler rules the judgement be
This day to judge and examine
Today is examination day
Too long delayed but yet
Are you too blind to the evils of non-discrimination
That you dare not understand?
Are you so willfully ignorant of what you should be;
That you think you are only what others say you are,
Yet perhaps you fail to realize
That what you are
you are
And thus so.
Thusly, if what you reap is what you so
What you reap is what you are:
Amen!
Because what you 'am' is what you be
And what you is, you am
And what you be, you are
If what you are is what you so.

* Recited by Sun Ra on the A&M CD "Purple Night" before the piece, "Of Invisible Them".

When Angels Speak

When angels speak
They speak of cosmic waves of sound
Wavelength infinity
Always touching planets
In opposition outward bound.

When angels speak
They speak on wavelength infinity
Beam cosmos
Synchronizing the rays of black darkness
Into visible being
Blackout!
Dark Living Myth-world of being.

Wisdom-Ignorance (IE Vol.1, 1972)

When reality reaches a certain point
Beyond that point is myth.
Even before the beginning of what is
called reality
Myth is the being before.
When all that is parable-possible
Is lived and caused to be, the hope
Of continuation-living-being is myth
Myth from equational wisdom-ignorance is.

     The myth is the seemingly false
and the seemingly impossible. The
borders of the realm of myth are vast
and nonexistent because
There is no limit to the imaginative
realm-idea of the myth.

     Here is a challenging frontier.
Only the bold and wise/ignorant
should pioneer. The law in the realm
of myth is the non-law to non-
mythist because the realm of the myth
is the magic presentation of the non-
existent non-reality in a seemingly
real form for it is when it is, and
yet when it is, it is not.

     The myth touches every field
of endeavor so that the myth is the
bridge to the Greater Myth.

     Out upon the planes of Myth
strange non-realities dwell,
strange because they are not
according to the propagated accepted "law".

     The non-reality may sometimes
be expressed by the word "not".
Sometimes that which has reached an
end is considered as "not",
So that a problem is posed and a way
out difficulty at the same time.
Consider the three o's.

[Wisdom-Ignorance]

(Space Is The Place LP Jacket, 1972)

When reality reaches a certain point
Beyond that point is myth.
Even before the beginning of what is called reality
Myth is the being before.
When all that is parable-possible
Is lived and caused to be, the hope
Of continuation-living-being is myth
Myth from equational wisdom-ignorance
Is . . . is.
The myth is the seemingly false
And the seemingly impossible.
The borders of the realm of myth are vast
And nonexistent because
There is no limit to the imaginative realm-idea of the myth.
Here is a challengingly frontier.

Words (1972)

. = aim
. = end
. - period
. = time
. = era
. = age
. = cycle

Words

Words are like people
They move many ways and cause many things to happen
A word is a name
A word when spoken is a sound
A word when thought is a vibration
There are good words and bad words
But any word can be good and any word can be bad
It is according to who says it and how and where and when and
why.
Words.

Words (1980)

Words are like people
    And people are like words . . . . . .
        They say the word was made flesh . . . .
        Yes . . . words are like people.
        They move many ways and cause many things to happen . . .
            A word is a name
                A word when spoken is a sound
                    A word when thought is a vibration . . . . .
                    There are good words
                        And there are bad words . . . .
                    But any word can be good
                    And any word can be bad,
                It is according to who says it and how
                    And where . . . . . and when . . . . and why.
                    Words are more than words are . . . .

Words And The Impossible

The elasticity of words
The phonetic - dimension of words
The multi-self of words
Is energy for thought - If it is a reality.
  The idea that words
Can form themselves into the impossible
Then the way to the impossible
Is through the words.

The fate of humanity is determined
By the word they so or approve
Because they reap what they so
Even if it is the fruit of their lies.

Would I For All That Were (1968)

Would I for all that were
If all that were is like a wish.
Would I for all that were
If all that were is that which never came to be;
For the image of the world that was
Is the light of the darkness today . . .
And all that were is not what I wish it were.
So would I for all that were
All that swirls anon in the world of dreams
Boundless in thought to fruitful reminisce.
Would I for all that were
All that words cannot express
All that pleasant dreams cannot remember . . .
The enchantment and warmth of rare content.
Would I for these and these alone
That I might live as Cosmic thought insists I should
As it were right to be as I wish I were.
Would I for this wondrous thing
A new decree of happiness
Better than, any liberty this world has ever known.
A Cosmic weigh
That opens the way to the worlds that are: --
The Kosmos worlds of endless galaxies.

Would I For All That Were (1972)

Would I for all that were
If all that were is like a wish
Would I for all that were
If all that were is that which never came to be
For the image of the world that was
Is the light of the darkness today
And all that were is not what I wish it were
All that swirls anon in the world of dreams
Boundless in thought and fruitful reminisce.

Would I for all that were
All that words cannot express
All that pleasant dreams cannot remember
The enchantment and warmth of rare content
Would I for these and these alone
That I might live as cosmic thought insists I should
As it were right to be as I wish to were.

Would I for this splendid thing
A different decree of hapiness
Better than any liberty this world has ever known.

Would I for all that were
That I might live as I were to be
That I might live as I would to should

Would I for all that were before the law of the oath of earth
The destructive chosen truth that led astray
Into a past-eternity
Disguised as the only future
So that those who love would love in vain

So that those who sought to live
Would seek in vain
So that those who dared to die
Did die in vain
All are chained to the idea of the past-eternity
Which came to pass in order that it be the past

Thus it came to past that it might tempt the earth
To be its own.

Would I for all that were
As before the realm of once I am
Before the beginning of the time of now
Before there was/the idea
Of the enacted play-on-words

Upon the tree the symbol would
And that is why: a sleeping world/
Lies enchanted by the word of the would-was of the woulding-tree
In the forest of wood-illusion.

Would I For All That Were (1980)

Would I for all that were
        If all that were is like a wish . . . .
Would I for all that were
        If all that were is that which never came to be.
      For the image of the world that was
      Is the light of the darkness today;
        And all that was is not what I wish it were.

Would I for all that were: All that words cannot express;
All that swirls anon in the world of dreams . . . .
        Boundless in thought and fruitful reminisce,
      All that pleasant dreams cannot remember:
    The enchantment and warmth of rare content.
    Would I for these and these alone
      That I might be as cosmic thought insists I should,
    As it were ideal-meant to be as I wish to were.

Would I for this splendid thing:
      A different decree-happiness;
      Better than any liberty this world has ever known
Would I for all that were . . That I might live as I were to be
    That I might live as I would to should
Would I for all that were before the law of sin earth-oath
    The destructive chosen truth that lead astray
             Into a past-cycle-eternity
        Which came to pass
        In order that it be the past.
        Thus it came to pass to be passed
      That it might tempt the earth to be it's own.

Would I for all that were as before the realm of once I am;
Before the beginning of the time of now . . . . . .
    Before there was the idea
      Of the enacted play-on-words upon the tree
      By symbol would . . . .
The enigma why:
    The world lies sleeping
    Enchanted by the word of the would was
      Of the woulding-tree
        In the forest of wood-illusion.

You Must Choose! (1972)

A widening of concepts is necessary
Another look at the future is required
Look and see the twin road vision light
It is darker than the night
It is the twin-road heraldry
Vibrations of a different kind . . . .
These kind vibrations kind are just the kind we need
The distance narrows
We are approaching the twin roads of the future
One day the planet earth must choose to change
And you must choose
There is no other way
Don't forget the alter hints I give to you . . . .
One day soon you must choose to change
Be sure your intuition's voice is not defied
Or perhaps neglectfully denied.
No other voice will speak to you
No other voice knows what to say . . . . . .

You Must Choose (1980)

A widening of concepts is necessary
　Another look at the future is required.
Look and see the twin road vision light
　　It is darker than the night . . . .
It is the twin-road heraldry
. . . . Vibrations of a different kind . . . . . .
　These kind vibrations are just the kind we need . . . . .

The distance narrows
We are approaching the twin roads of the future . . . . . .
One day the planet earth must choose to change
. . . . Yes . . . . .
There is no other way.
　　　Don't forget the alter hints I give to you . . . .
　　　　The day is soon that you must choose to change . . .
　　　Be sure your intuitions voice is not denied
　　　Or perhaps unintentionally defied . . . .
　　　No other voice will speak to you
　　　There is nothing left for any other voice to say.

Circa 1964

"I Have A Gift To Offer..." (c. 1978)[1]

"I have a gift to offer this planet and music is one of the bridges to the treasure house of it. I am doing what I am supposed to do, I am being what I came here to be. Those who are in tune with Nature can hear what those who are not in tune cannot hear, and then they will know the meaning of the natural beist. The space sea has many sounds of beistness. The Akasa, the unknown acoustics, the alter-planes of isness are all a part of everything, the everything and the nothingness of Space Outer."

The Impossible (1965)[2]

"The impossible is the watchword of the greater space age" The space age cannot be avoided and the SPACE MUSIC is the key to understanding the meaning of the IMPOSSIBLE and every other enigma.

---

1 This prose piece, extracted from "My Music Is Words" is printed on the back of "Song of the Stargazers" LP and in a Saturn brochure available c. 1978. It later became a portion of the 1972 version of "The Universe Sent Me To Converse With You".
2 Printed on the "Interstellar Low Ways" LP jacket. The original text is in all capitals, with certain words in a larger font (given here as all caps.)

"In This Age..."

In this age of Outer Space challenge, People will have to change their tune, i.e. they will have to be tuned up or down (according to what is necessary) another way. The intergalactic counsil has a different tuning system. The insistent idea is that people will have to change their tune and that tuning should be in tune with the intergalactic outer universe which is everything which is not yet in. And this is the meaning of the Kingdom of not and its phonetic note. Note!

This is about note and notes. Notes are written messages which can be conveyed into sound. So that the kingdom of sound is an equational similarity to the kingdom of notes which in this case is the music but the music of not touches upon the realm of myth of the outer-alter potential . . . The eternal endless mythology spectrum hieroglyphic parallel/duology presence.

This music is about multiplicity and simplicity of paradox when the code is known. Sometimes the threads from the inner not/myth are woven into the fabric of infinity sound presentation for the sake of comparison enlightenment revelation.

Its is about nature and its equational beauty/transcendent art.

To me this music is of discipline-form because freedom is an earth deviation futility if it is of the stumbling block variety. Take care!

This music is blueprint/declaration of different kinds of potentials.

The myth is not but not is the future potential . . . as I said, phonetic differentials point to another kind of world . . . for instance something that has already been . . . you could say that's not, but something that has never been, you could say that's not . . . so I would say that the future that you know nothing of is not . . . This is of the differential evaluation.

> The primary enigma is the being and the been as
> to differntial relationship . . .
> That which been: isn't
> And that which be: is
> These are the words of the future
> From the cosmic law
> Of the united worlds.
> That turn like jewels in the eternal sky
>
> Thus it is spoken and thus it is.

What is PHAELOS?

PHAELOS (fy-los) is derived from the Greek, *philos* that means fondness, and loving. Phaelos is a natural quality and expression of humanity that we believe is not necessarily in short supply, but under-utilized in our society.

Phaelos Books and Mediawerks was inspired by a vision of, and desire for a better world made possible by *conscious,* loving choice — one mind and heart at a time — through self-reliance and positive cooperation among people.

CELEBRATE SUN RA!

Share the legend and legacy of Sun Ra with others through these custom designed, high quality commemorative products.

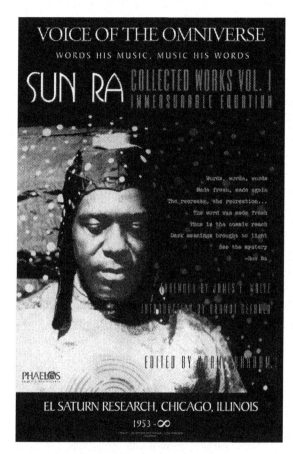

SRCW-P001, 25 x 38 in. $39.95

Sun Ra "Voice of the Omniverse" Poster
Product No. SRCW-P001, 25 x 38 in., $39.95
— Inspired by the cover art to Sun Ra's book of poetry. Honors the beginning of Ra's association with Alton Abraham and El Saturn Research in Chicago, Illinois.

Sun Ra "Voice of the Omniverse" T-Shirt
Product No. SCRW-T001, Gilden Ultra Cotton Heavyweight. 100% preshrunk heavyweight cotton, 6.1 oz., seamless collar, taped neck and shoulders, double-needle throughout. $16.95 — Available in S-XXXXL. (3XL and 4XL add $2.00).

SRCW-T001, T-Shirt $16.95

Available online at phaelos.com

Additional Titles from Phaelos Books

Available online at phaelos.com

I Am My Body, NOT!

ISBN 0-9700209-1-0, 60 ppg., hardcover, $19.95 — Written by Adam Abraham, illustrated by Marie Litster. The comprehensive introduction to the workings of the human body is really only a beneficial by-product of this groundbreaking book. It's real value lies in the consistent, conscious, and loving message that it sends about the importance of love, permanence of life, and of who we are.

A Freed Man: An Emancipation Proclamation

ISBN 0-9700209-0-2, 304 ppg. softcover, $17.95 — Written by Adam Abraham. A collection of twenty-one essays that present a blueprint for positive individual and social change, beginning within, through what the author calls Wonderful Dreams.

I Am Spirit!

ISBN 0-9700209-3-7, 80 ppg., hardcover, $22.95 — Written by Adam Abraham, illustrated by Marie Litster. Picks up where *I Am My Body, NOT!* leaves off. A dramatically designed and lovingly written and illustrated poem that pegs our beginnings in the heavens, and our ultimate aim (not end), as love.

My Soul's Shadow

MSS-020414, 11 x 17 in., $11.95 — A hauntingly personal poem written by Adam Abraham that embraces the depths of human experience with a clear awareness of the ever present Light that guides and enfolds us. Printed on premium quality semi-gloss, UV coated paper, suitable for framing.

Love Proclamations

LPO-2002-1, Our Love, LPI-2002-2 My Love, and LPF-2002-3, Our Family's Love, $11.95 ea. — Written by Adam Abraham, Love Proclamations!™ are an effective way for individuals, couples, groups, organizations and families to officially establish and affirm the "ground rules" of healthy behavior and relationship, each to the other, and with one's self.

Love Proclamations

Take a closer look at the text sample below. Other versions are available for any form of relationship with others (romantic, personal, or business), and within a family. Signature, witness, and date lines are included at the end.

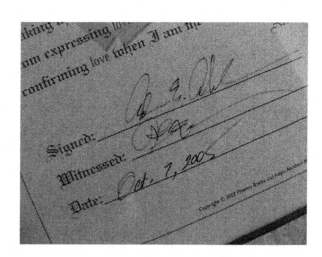

Proclamation Of "My" Love

Let it be proclaimed and agreed that I will practice and observe only one acceptable "standard" of behavior... one based on, and in, love; that begins with "me".

I hereby proclaim that love shall be the foundation for, and energy behind, my relationships. That love shall be the motive, reason, quality, and method that lives *within* each thought, word, action, and deed that comes from "me".

I furthemore proclaim that respect — for myself and others — is an implicit, omnipresent, and integral element of love, and therefore, I will practice respect for self even in the absence of "loving feelings." I understand that truth is the cornerstone of trust, and that both will serve as indicators of the health and strength of my love, even when I am "alone."

I proclaim and agree that love cannot be faked. I consciously choose it and give it willingly, and regularly — to myself and others — even if I don't receive love from others in kind.

Making this Proclamation does not absolve or relieve me from expressing love verbally, or from the privilege of openly confirming love when I am the recipient of such expressions.

                    And so, let love be done.

LPI-02002-2

Contact Information

Phaelos Books & Mediawerks
860 N. McQueen Rd #1171
Chandler, AZ 85225-8104

480.275.4925
509.479.8415 (fax)

www.phaelos.com
info@phaelos.com

Reseller inquiries are welcomed.

231

CPSIA information can be obtained
at www.ICGtesting.com
Printed in the USA
BVOW09s0511141116

467748BV00018B/107/P